Machine Learning with
Quick Start Guide

Hands-on techniques for building supervised and unsupervised machine learning workflows

Michael Bironneau
Toby Coleman

Packt>

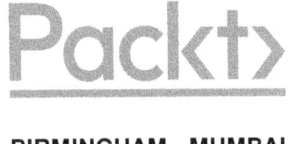

BIRMINGHAM - MUMBAI

Machine Learning with Go Quick Start Guide

Copyright © 2019 Packt Publishing

All rights reserved. No part of this book may be reproduced, stored in a retrieval system, or transmitted in any form or by any means, without the prior written permission of the publisher, except in the case of brief quotations embedded in critical articles or reviews.

Every effort has been made in the preparation of this book to ensure the accuracy of the information presented. However, the information contained in this book is sold without warranty, either express or implied. Neither the authors, nor Packt Publishing or its dealers and distributors, will be held liable for any damages caused or alleged to have been caused directly or indirectly by this book.

Packt Publishing has endeavored to provide trademark information about all of the companies and products mentioned in this book by the appropriate use of capitals. However, Packt Publishing cannot guarantee the accuracy of this information.

Commissioning Editor: Amey Varangaonkar
Acquisition Editor: Aditi Gour
Content Development Editor: Roshan Kumar
Technical Editor: Sagar Sawant
Copy Editor: Safis Editing
Project Coordinator: Namrata Swetta
Proofreader: Safis Editing
Indexer: Manju Arasan
Graphics: Jisha Chirayil
Production Coordinator: Aparna Bhagat

First published: May 2019

Production reference: 1310519

Published by Packt Publishing Ltd.
Livery Place
35 Livery Street
Birmingham
B3 2PB, UK.

ISBN 978-1-83855-035-6

www.packtpub.com

mapt.io

Mapt is an online digital library that gives you full access to over 5,000 books and videos, as well as industry leading tools to help you plan your personal development and advance your career. For more information, please visit our website.

Why subscribe?

- Spend less time learning and more time coding with practical eBooks and Videos from over 4,000 industry professionals

- Improve your learning with Skill Plans built especially for you

- Get a free eBook or video every month

- Mapt is fully searchable

- Copy and paste, print, and bookmark content

Packt.com

Did you know that Packt offers eBook versions of every book published, with PDF and ePub files available? You can upgrade to the eBook version at www.packt.com and as a print book customer, you are entitled to a discount on the eBook copy. Get in touch with us at customercare@packtpub.com for more details.

At www.packt.com, you can also read a collection of free technical articles, sign up for a range of free newsletters, and receive exclusive discounts and offers on Packt books and eBooks.

Contributors

About the authors

Michael Bironneau is an award-winning mathematician and experienced software engineer. He holds a PhD in mathematics from Loughborough University and has worked in several data science and software development roles. He is currently technical director of the energy AI technology company, Open Energi.

Toby Coleman is an experienced data science and machine learning practitioner. Following degrees from Cambridge University and Imperial College London, he has worked on the application of data science techniques in the banking and energy sectors. Recently, he held the position of innovation director at cleantech SME Open Energi, and currently provides machine learning consultancy to start-up businesses.

About the reviewers

Niclas Jern has been using computers for fun and profit since he got his first computer (a C64) at the age of four. After a prolonged period of combining the founding and running of a start-up, Walkbase, with his university studies, he graduated from Åbo Akademi University with an M.Sc. in computer engineering in 2015. His hobbies include long walks, lifting heavy metal objects at the gym, and spending quality time with his wife and daughter. He currently works at Stratacache, which acquired Walkbase in 2017, where he continues to lead the Walkbase engineering teams and design and build the future of retail technology.

Philipp Mieden is a German security researcher and software engineer, currently focusing on network security monitoring with applied machine learning. He presented his research on classifying malicious behavior in network traffic at several international contests and conferences and won multiple prizes. He holds a B.Sc. degree from the Ludwig Maximilian University of Munich, and shares many of his projects on GitHub. Besides network anomaly detection, Philipp is also interested in hardware security, industrial control systems, and reverse engineering malware.

Packt is searching for authors like you

If you're interested in becoming an author for Packt, please visit `authors.packtpub.com` and apply today. We have worked with thousands of developers and tech professionals, just like you, to help them share their insight with the global tech community. You can make a general application, apply for a specific hot topic that we are recruiting an author for, or submit your own idea.

Table of Contents

Preface 1

Chapter 1: Introducing Machine Learning with Go 5
  What is ML? 6
  Types of ML algorithms 7
    Supervised learning problems 8
    Unsupervised learning problems 9
  Why write ML applications in Go? 9
    The advantages of Go 9
    Go's mature ecosystem 10
    Transfer knowledge and models created in other languages 11
  ML development life cycle 11
    Defining problem and objectives 12
    Acquiring and exploring data 13
    Selecting the algorithm 14
    Preparing data 15
    Training 16
    Validating/testing 17
    Integrating and deploying 18
    Re-validating 18
  Summary 19
  Further readings 19

Chapter 2: Setting Up the Development Environment 21
  Installing Go 22
    Linux, macOS, and FreeBSD 22
    Windows 23
  Running Go interactively with gophernotes 23
  Example – the most common phrases in positive and negative reviews 25
    Initializing the example directory and downloading the dataset 25
    Loading the dataset files 26
    Parsing contents into a Struct 27
    Loading the data into a Gota dataframe 29
    Finding the most common phrases 30
  Example – exploring body mass index data with gonum/plot 32
    Installing gonum and gonum/plot 32
    Loading the data 33
    Understanding the distributions of the data series 34
  Example – preprocessing data with Gota 37

Loading the data into Gota	38
Removing and renaming columns	39
Converting a column into a different type	40
Filtering out unwanted data	41
Normalizing the Height, Weight, and Age columns	42
Sampling to obtain training/validation subsets	45
Encoding data with categorical variables	47
Summary	**50**
Further readings	**51**
Chapter 3: Supervised Learning	**53**
Classification	**54**
A simple model – the logistic classifier	56
Measuring performance	59
Precision and recall	59
ROC curves	62
Multi-class models	63
A non-linear model – the support vector machine	66
Overfitting and underfitting	69
Deep learning	70
Neural networks	71
A simple deep learning model architecture	73
Neural network training	74
Regression	**75**
Linear regression	78
Random forest regression	79
Other regression models	80
Summary	**80**
Further readings	**81**
Chapter 4: Unsupervised Learning	**83**
Clustering	**84**
Principal component analysis	**88**
Summary	**91**
Further readings	**91**
Chapter 5: Using Pretrained Models	**93**
How to restore a saved GoML model	**94**
Deciding when to adopt a polyglot approach	**95**
Example – invoking a Python model using os/exec	**97**
Example – invoking a Python model using HTTP	**100**
Example – deep learning using the TensorFlow API for Go	**102**
Installing TensorFlow	104
Import the pretrained TensorFlow model	106
Creating inputs to the TensorFlow model	108
Summary	**110**

| Further readings | 110 |

Chapter 6: Deploying Machine Learning Applications — 113
The continuous delivery feedback loop — 113
- Developing — 114
- Testing — 114
- Deployment — 116
  - Dependencies — 116
  - Model persistence — 119
- Monitoring — 121
  - Structured logging — 123
  - Capturing metrics — 124
  - Feedback — 125

Deployment models for ML applications — 128
- Infrastructure-as-a-service — 128
  - Amazon Web Services — 129
  - Microsoft Azure — 129
  - Google Cloud — 130
- Platform-as-a-Service — 131
  - Amazon Web Services — 131
    - Amazon Sagemaker — 131
    - Amazon AI Services — 132
  - Microsoft Azure — 133
    - Azure ML Studio — 134
    - Azure Cognitive Services — 134
  - Google Cloud — 134
    - AI Platform — 135
    - AI Building Blocks — 135

Summary — 137
Further readings — 137

Chapter 7: Conclusion - Successful ML Projects — 141
When to use ML — 142
Typical stages in a ML project — 144
- Business and data understanding — 145
- Data preparation — 145
- Modelling and evaluation — 146
- Deployment — 147

When to combine ML with traditional code — 147
Summary — 148
Further readings — 148

Other Books You May Enjoy — 149

Index — 153

Preface

Machine learning (**ML**) plays a vital part in the modern data-driven world, and has been extensively adopted in various fields across financial forecasting, effective searching, robotics, digital imaging in healthcare, and many more besides. It is a rapidly evolving field, with new algorithms and datasets being published every week, both by academics and technology companies. This book will teach you how to perform various machine learning tasks using Go in different environments.

You will learn about many important techniques that are required to develop ML applications in Go, and deploy them as production systems. The best way to develop your knowledge is with hands-on experience, so dive in and start adding ML software to your own Go applications.

Who this book is for

This book is intended for developers and data scientists with at least a beginner-level knowledge of Go, and a vague idea of what types of problems ML aims to tackle. No advanced knowledge of Go, or a theoretical understanding of the mathematics that underpins ML, is required.

What this book covers

`Chapter 1`, *Introducing Machine Learning with Go*, introduces ML and the different types of ML-related problems. We will also look into the ML development life cycle, and the process of creating and taking an ML application to production.

`Chapter 2`, *Setting Up the Development Environment*, explains how to set up an environment for ML applications and Go. We will also gain an understanding of how to install an interactive environment, Jupyter, to accelerate data exploration and visualization using libraries such as Gota and gonum/plot.

`Chapter 3`, *Supervised Learning*, introduces supervised learning algorithms and demonstrates how to choose an ML algorithm, train it, and validate its predictive power on previously unseen data.

Preface

Chapter 4, *Unsupervised Learning*, reuses many of the techniques related to data loading and preparation that we have implemented in this book, but will focuses instead on unsupervised machine learning.

Chapter 5, *Using Pretrained Models*, describes how to load a pretrained Go ML model and use it to generate a prediction. We will also gain an understanding of how to use HTTP to invoke ML models written in other languages, where they may reside on a different machine or even on the internet.

Chapter 6, *Deploying Machine Learning Applications*, covers the final stage of the ML development life cycle: taking an ML application written in Go to production.

Chapter 7, *Conclusion – Successful ML Projects*, takes a step back and examines ML development from a project management point of view.

To get the most out of this book

The code samples, including bash scripts and installation instructions, were tested on an Ubuntu 16.04 server with 8 GB of RAM and a 500 GB SSD hard drive. A machine with similar specifications will be required.

Download the example code files

You can download the example code files for this book from your account at www.packt.com. If you purchased this book elsewhere, you can visit www.packt.com/support and register to have the files emailed directly to you.

You can download the code files by following these steps:

1. Log in or register at www.packt.com.
2. Select the **SUPPORT** tab.
3. Click on **Code Downloads & Errata**.
4. Enter the name of the book in the **Search** box and follow the onscreen instructions.

Once the file is downloaded, please make sure that you unzip or extract the folder using the latest version of:

- WinRAR/7-Zip for Windows
- Zipeg/iZip/UnRarX for Mac
- 7-Zip/PeaZip for Linux

The code bundle for the book is also hosted on GitHub at `https://github.com/PacktPublishing/Machine-Learning-with-Go-Quick-Start-Guide`. In case there's an update to the code, it will be updated on the existing GitHub repository.

We also have other code bundles from our rich catalog of books and videos available at `https://github.com/PacktPublishing/`. Check them out!

Download the color images

We also provide a PDF file that has color images of the screenshots/diagrams used in this book. You can download it here: `http://www.packtpub.com/sites/default/files/downloads/9781838550356_ColorImages.pdf`.

Conventions used

There are a number of text conventions used throughout this book.

`CodeInText`: Indicates code words in text, database table names, folder names, filenames, file extensions, pathnames, dummy URLs, user input, and Twitter handles. Here is an example: "The `go-deep` library lets us build this architecture very quickly."

A block of code is set as follows:

```
categories := []string{"tshirt", "trouser", "pullover", "dress", "coat",
"sandal", "shirt", "shoe", "bag", "boot"}
```

Bold: Indicates a new term, an important word, or words that you see on screen. For example, words in menus or dialog boxes appear in the text like this. Here is an example: "Create a new Notebook by clicking on **New** | **Go**:"

Warnings or important notes appear like this.

Tips and tricks appear like this.

Get in touch

Feedback from our readers is always welcome.

General feedback: If you have questions about any aspect of this book, mention the book title in the subject of your message and email us at `customercare@packtpub.com`.

Errata: Although we have taken every care to ensure the accuracy of our content, mistakes do happen. If you have found a mistake in this book, we would be grateful if you would report this to us. Please visit `www.packt.com/submit-errata`, selecting your book, clicking on the Errata Submission Form link, and entering the details.

Piracy: If you come across any illegal copies of our works in any form on the internet, we would be grateful if you would provide us with the location address or website name. Please contact us at `copyright@packt.com` with a link to the material.

If you are interested in becoming an author: If there is a topic that you have expertise in, and you are interested in either writing or contributing to a book, please visit `authors.packtpub.com`.

Reviews

Please leave a review. Once you have read and used this book, why not leave a review on the site that you purchased it from? Potential readers can then see and use your unbiased opinion to make purchase decisions, we at Packt can understand what you think about our products, and our authors can see your feedback on their book. Thank you!

For more information about Packt, please visit `packt.com`.

1
Introducing Machine Learning with Go

All around us, automation is changing our lives in subtle increments that live on the bleeding edge of mathematics and computer science. What do a Nest thermostat, Netflix's movie recommendations and Google's Images search algorithm all have in common? Created by some of the brightest minds in todays software industry, these technologies all rely on **machine learning** (**ML**) techniques.

In February 2019, Crunchbase listed over 4,700 companies that categorized themselves as **Artificial Intelligence** (**AI**) or ML[1]. Most of these companies were very early stage and funded by angel investors or early round funding from venture capitalists. Yet articles in 2017 and 2018 by Crunchbase, and the UK Financial Times, center around a common recognition that ML is increasingly relied upon for sustained growth[2], and that its increasing maturity will lead to even more widespread applications[3], particularly if challenges around the opacity of decisions made by ML algorithms can be solved[4]. The New York Times even has a column dedicated to ML[5], a tribute to its importance in everyday life.

This book will teach a software engineer with intermediate knowledge of the Go programming language how to write and produce an ML application from concept to deployment, and beyond. We will first categorize problems suitable for ML techniques and the life cycle of ML applications. Then, we will explain how to set up a development environment specifically suited for data science with the Go language. Then, we will provide a practical guide to the main ML algorithms, their implementations, and their pitfalls. We will also provide some guidance on using ML models produced using other programming languages and integrating them in Go applications. Finally, we will consider different deployment models and the elusive intersection between DevOps and data science. We will conclude with some remarks on managing ML projects from our own experience.

Introducing Machine Learning with Go

 ML theory is a mathematically advanced subject, but you can develop ML applications without fully understanding it. This book will help you develop an intuition for which algorithms to use and how to formulate problems with only basic mathematical knowledge.

In our first chapter, we will introduce some fundamental concepts of Go ML applications:

- What is ML?
- Types of ML problems
- Why write ML applications in Go?
- The ML development life cycle

What is ML?

ML is a field at the intersection of statistics and computer science. The output of this field has been a collection of algorithms capable of operating autonomously by inferring the best decision or answer to a question from a dataset. Unlike traditional programming, where the programmer must decide the rules of the program and painstakingly encode these in the syntax of their chosen programming language, ML algorithms require only sufficient quantities of prepared data, computing power to learn from the data, and often some knowledge to tweak the algorithms parameters to improve the final result.

The resulting systems are very flexible and can be excellent at capitalizing on patterns that human beings would miss. Imagine writing a recommender system for a TV series from scratch. Perhaps you might begin by defining the inputs and the outputs of the problem, then finding a database of TV series that had such details as their date of release, genre, cast, and director. Finally, you might create a `score` func that rates a pair of series more highly if their release dates are close, they have the same genre, share actors, or have the same director.

 A **recommender system** is a type of prediction algorithm that attempts to guess the rating a user would ascribe an input sample. A widely used application in online retail is to use a recommender system to suggest items to a user, based on their past purchases.

Given one TV series, you could then rank all other TV series by decreasing similarity score and present the first few to the user. When creating the `score` func, you would make judgement calls on the relative importance of the various features, such as deciding that each pair of shared actors between two series is worth one point. This type of guesswork, also known as a **heuristic**, is what ML algorithms aim to do for you, saving time and improving the accuracy of the final result, especially if user preferences shift and you have to change the scoring func regularly to keep up.

The distinction between the broader field of AI and ML is a murky one. While the hype surrounding ML may be relatively new[6], the history of the field began in 1959 when Arthur Samuel, a leading expert in AI, first used these words[7]. In the 1950s, ML concepts such as the perceptron and genetic algorithms were invented by the likes of Alan Turing[8] as well as Samuel himself. In the following decades, practical and theoretical difficulties in achieving general AI, led to approaches such as rule-based methods such as expert systems, which did not learn from data, but rather from expert-devised rules which they had learned over many years, encoded in if-else statements.

 The power of ML is in the ability of the algorithms to adapt to previously unseen cases, something that if-else statements cannot do. If you do not require this adaptability, perhaps because all cases are known beforehand, stick to basics and use traditional programming techniques instead!

In the 1990s, recognizing that achieving AI was unlikely with existing technology, there was an increasing appetite for a narrow approach to tackling very specific problems that could be solved using a combination of statistics and probability theory. This led to the development of ML as a separate field. Today, ML and AI are often used interchangeably, particularly in marketing literature[9].

Types of ML algorithms

There are two main categories of ML algorithms: supervised learning and unsupervised learning. The decision of which type of algorithm to use depends on the data you have available and the project objectives.

Supervised learning problems

Supervised learning problems aim to infer the best mapping between an input and output dataset based on provided labeled pairs of input/output. The labeled dataset acts as feedback for the algorithm, allowing it to gauge the optimality of its solution. For example, given a list of mean yearly crude oil prices from 2010-2018, you may wish to predict the mean yearly crude oil price of 2019. The error that the algorithm makes on the 2010-2018 years will allow the engineer to estimate its error on the target prediction year of 2019.

A **labeled pair** consists of an input vector consisting of independent variables and an output vector consisting of dependent variables. For example, a labeled dataset for facial recognition might contain input vectors with facial image data alongside output vectors encoding the photographed persons name. A **labeled set** (or dataset) is a collection of labeled pairs.

Given a labeled collection of handwritten digits, you may wish to predict the label of a previously unseen handwritten digit. Similarly, given a dataset of emails that are labeled as being either spam or not spam, a company that wants to create a spam filter would want to predict whether a previously unseen message was spam. All these problems are supervised learning problems.

Supervised ML problems can be further divided into prediction and classification:

- Classification attempts to label an unknown input sample with a known output value. For example, you could train an algorithm to recognize breeds of cats. The algorithm would classify an unknown cat by labeling it with a known breed.
- By contrast, prediction algorithms attempt to label an unknown input sample with either a known or unknown output value. This is also known as **estimation** or **regression**. A canonical prediction problem is time series forecasting, where the output value of the series is predicted for a time value that was not previously seen.

A **classification algorithm** will try to associate an input sample with an item from a given list of output categories: for example, deciding whether a photo represents a cat, a dog, or neither is a classification problem. A **prediction algorithm** will map an input sample to a member of an output domain, which could be continuous: for example, attempting to guess a persons height from their weight and gender would be a prediction problem.

We will cover supervised algorithms in more detail in Chapter 3, *Supervised Learning*.

Unsupervised learning problems

Unsupervised learning problems aim to learn from data that has not been labeled. For example, given a dataset of market research data, a clustering algorithm can divide consumers into segments, saving time for marketing professionals. Given a dataset of medical scans, unsupervised classification algorithms can divide the image between different kinds of tissues for further analysis. One unsupervised learning approach known as dimensionality reduction works in conjunction with other algorithms, as a pre-processing step, to reduce the volume of data that another algorithm will have to be trained on, cutting down training times. We will cover unsupervised learning algorithms in more detail in `Chapter 4`, *Unsupervised Learning*.

Most ML algorithms can be efficiently implemented in a wide range of programming languages. While Python has been a favorite of data scientists for its ease of use and plethora of open source libraries, Go presents significant advantages for a developer creating a commercial ML application.

Why write ML applications in Go?

There are libraries for other languages, especially Python, that are more complete than Go ML libraries and have benefited from years, if not decades, of research from the worlds brightest brains. Some Go programmers make the transition to Go in search of better performance, but because ML libraries are typically written in C and exposed to Python through their bindings, they do not suffer the same performance problems as interpreted Python programs. Deep learning frameworks such as TensorFlow and Caffe have very limited, if any, bindings to Go. Even with these issues in mind, Go is still an excellent, if not the best, language to develop an application containing ML components.

The advantages of Go

For researchers attempting to improve state-of-the-art algorithms in an academic environment, Go may not be the best choice. However, for a start-up with a product concept and fast-dwindling cash reserves, completing the development of the product in a maintainable and reliable way within a short space of time is essential, and this is where the Go language shines.

Go (or Golang) originates from Google, where its design began in 2007[10]. Its stated objectives were to create an efficient, compiled programming language that feels lightweight and pleasant[11]. Go benefits from a number of features that are designed to boost productivity and reliability of production applications:

- Easy to learn and on-board new developers
- Fast build time
- Good performance at run-time
- Great concurrency support
- Excellent standard library
- Type safety
- Easy-to-read, standardized code with `gofmt`
- Forced error handling to minimize unforeseen exceptions
- Explicit, clear dependency management
- Easy to adapt architecture as projects grow

All these reasons make Go an excellent language for building production systems, particularly web applications. The 2018 Stack Overflow developer survey reveals that while only 7% of professional developers use Go as their main language, it is 5th on the most loved list and also commands very high salaries relative to other languages, recognizing the business value that Go programmers add[12].

Go's mature ecosystem

Some of the worlds most successful technology companies use Go as the main language of their production systems and actively contribute to its development, such as Cloudflare[13], Google, Uber[14], Dailymotion[15], and Medium[16]. This means that there is now an extensive ecosystem of tools and libraries to help a development team create a reliable, maintainable application in Go. Even Docker, the worlds leading container technology, is written in Go.

At the time of writing, there are 1,774 repositories on GitHub written in the Go language that have over 500 stars, traditionally considered a good proxy measure of quality and support. In comparison, Python has 3,811 and Java 3,943. Considering that Go is several decades younger and allows for faster production-ready development, the relatively large number of well-supported repositories written in the Go language constitutes a glowing endorsement from the open source community.

Go has a number of stable and well-supported open source ML libraries. The most popular Go ML library by number of GitHub stars and contributors is GoLearn[17]. It is also the most recently updated. Other Go ML libraries include GoML and Gorgonia, a deep learning library whose API resembles TensorFlow.

Transfer knowledge and models created in other languages

Data scientists will often explore different methods to tackle an ML problem in a different language, such as Python, and produce a model that can solve the problem outside any application. The plumbing, such as getting data in and out of the model, serving this to a customer, persisting outputs or inputs, logging errors, or monitoring latencies, is not part of this deliverable and is outside the normal scope of work for a data scientist. As a result, taking the model from concept to a Go production application requires a polyglot approach such as a microservice.

Most of the code examples in this book use ML algorithms or bindings to libraries such as OpenCV that are also available in languages such as Python. This will enable you to take a data scientists prototype Python code and turn it into a production Go application in no time.

However, there are Go bindings for deep learning frameworks such as TensorFlow and Caffe. Moreover, for more basic algorithms such as decision trees, the same algorithms have also been implemented in Go libraries and will produce the same results if they are configured in the same way. Together, these considerations imply that it is possible to fully integrate data science products into a Go application without sacrificing accuracy, speed, or forcing a data scientist to work with tools they are uncomfortable with.

ML development life cycle

The ML development life cycle is a process to create and take to production an application containing an ML model that solves a business problem. The ML model can then be served to customers through the application as part of a product or service offering.

The following diagram illustrates the ML development life cycle process:

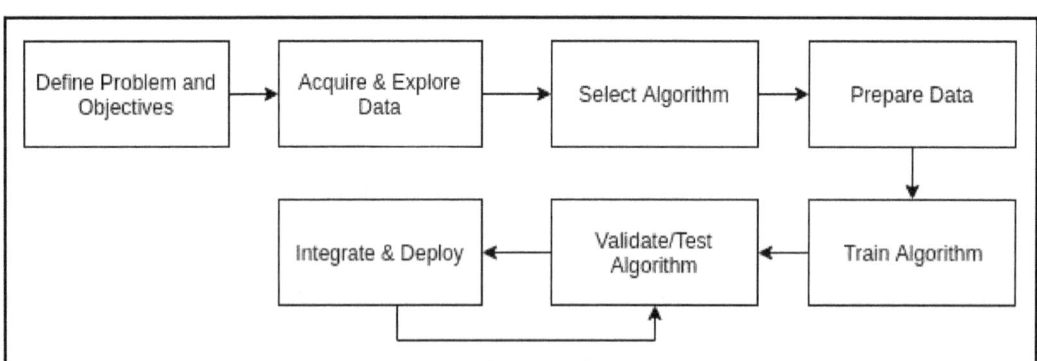

Defining problem and objectives

Before any development begins, the problem to be solved must be defined together with objectives of what good will look like, to set expectations. The way the problem is formulated is very important, as this can mean the difference between intractability and a simple solution. It is also likely to involve a conversation about where the input data for any algorithm will come from.

ML algorithms usually require large amounts of data to perform at their best. Sourcing quality data is the most important consideration when planning a ML project.

The typical formulation of an ML problem takes the form *given X dataset, predict Y*. The availability of data or lack of it thereof can affect the formulation of the problem, the solution, and its feasibility. For example, consider the problem *given a large labeled set of images of handwritten digits*[18]*, predict the label of a previously unseen image*. Deep learning algorithms have demonstrated that it is possible to achieve relatively high accuracy on this particular problem with little work on the part of the engineer, as long as the training dataset is sufficiently large[19]. If the training set is not large, the problem immediately becomes more difficult and requires a careful selection of the algorithm to use. It also affects the accuracy and thus, the set of attainable objectives.

Experiments performed by Michael Nielsen on the MNIST handwritten digit dataset show that the difference between training an ML algorithm with 1 example of labeled input/output pairs per digit and 5 examples was an improvement of accuracy from around 40% to around 65% for most algorithms tested[20]. Using 10 examples per digit usually raised the accuracy a further 5%.

If insufficient data is available to meet the project objectives, it is sometimes possible to boost performance by artificially expanding the dataset by making small changes to existing examples. In the previously mentioned experiments, Nielsen observed that adding slightly rotated or translated images to the dataset improved performance by as much as 15%.

Acquiring and exploring data

We argued earlier that it is critical to understand the input dataset before specifying project objectives, particularly objectives related to accuracy. As a general rule, ML algorithms will produce the best results when there are large training datasets available. The more data is used to train them, the better they will perform.

Acquiring data is, therefore, a key step in the ML development life cycle—one that can be very time-consuming and fraught with difficulty. In certain industries, privacy legislation may cause a lack of availability of personal data, making it difficult to create personalized products or requiring anonymization of source data before it can be used. Some datasets may be available but could require such extensive preparation or even manual labeling that it may put the project timeline or budget under stress.

Even if you do not have a proprietary dataset to apply to your problem, you may be able to find public datasets to use. Often, public datasets will have received attention from researchers, so you may find that the particular problem you are attempting to tackle has already been solved and the solution is open source. Some good sources of public datasets areas follows:

- **Awesome datasets**: https://github.com/awesomedata/awesome-public-datasets
- **Skymind open datasets**: https://skymind.ai/wiki/open-datasets
- **OpenML**: https://www.openml.org/
- **Kaggle**: https://www.kaggle.com/datasets
- **UK Governments open data**: https://data.gov.uk/
- **US Governments open data**: https://www.data.gov/

Once the dataset has been acquired, it should be explored to gain a basic understanding of how the different features (independent variables) may affect the desired output. For example, when attempting to predict correct height and weight from self-reported figures, researchers determined from initial exploration that older subjects were more likely to under-report obesity and therefore that age was thus a relevant feature when building their model. Attempting to build a model from all available data, even features that may not be relevant, can lead to longer training times in the best case, and can severely hamper accuracy in the worst case by introducing noise.

It is worth spending a bit more time to process and transform a dataset as this will improve the accuracy of the end result and maybe even the training time. All the code examples in this book include data processing and transformation.

In Chapter 2, *Setting Up the ML Environment*, we will see how to explore data using Go and an interactive browser-based tool called **Jupyter**.

Selecting the algorithm

The selection of the algorithm is arguably the most important decision that an ML application engineer will need to make, and the one that will take the most research. Sometimes, it is even required to combine an ML algorithm with traditional computer science algorithms to make a problem more tractable—an example of this is a recommender system that we consider later.

A good first step to start homing in on the best algorithm to solve a given problem is to determine whether a supervised or unsupervised approach is required. We introduced both earlier in the chapter. As a rule of thumb, when you are in possession of a labeled dataset and wish to categorize or predict a previously unseen sample, this will use a supervised algorithm. When you wish to understand an unlabeled dataset better by clustering it into different groups, possibly to then classify new samples against, you will use an unsupervised learning algorithm. A deeper understanding of the advantages and pitfalls of each algorithm and a thorough exploration of your data will provide enough information to select an algorithm. To help you get started, we cover a range of supervised learning algorithms in Chapter 3, *Supervised Learning*, and unsupervised learning algorithms in Chapter 4, *Unsupervised Learning*.

Some problems can lend themselves to a deft application of both ML techniques and traditional computer science. One such problem is recommender systems, which are now widespread in online retailers such as Amazon and Netflix. This problem asks, *given a dataset of each users set of purchased items, predict a set of N items that the user is most likely to purchase next*. This is exemplified in Amazons *people who buy X also buy Y* system.

The basic idea of the solution is that, if two users purchase very similar items, then any items not in the intersection of their purchased items are good candidates for their future purchases. First, transform the dataset so that it maps pairs of items to a score that expresses their co-occurrence. This can be computed by taking the number of times that the same customer has purchased both items, divided by the number of times a customer has purchased either one or the other, to give a number between 0 and 1. This now provides a labeled dataset to train a supervised algorithm such as a binary classifier to predict the score for a previously unseen pair. Combining this with a sorting algorithm can produce, given a single item, a list of items in a sorted rank of purchasability.

Preparing data

Data preparation refers to the processes performed on the input dataset before training the algorithm. A rigorous preparation process can simultaneously enhance the quality of the data and reduce the amount of time it will take the algorithm to reach the desired accuracy. The two steps to preparing data are data pre-processing and data transformation. We will go into more detail on preparing data in Chapters 2, *Setting Up The Development Environment*, Chapter 3, *Supervised Learning*, and Chapter 4, *Unsupervised Learning*.

Data pre-processing aims to transform the input dataset into a format that is adequate for work with the selected algorithm. A typical example of a pre-processing task is to format a date column in a certain way, or to ingest CSV files into a database, discarding any rows that lead to parsing errors. There may also be missing data values in an input data file that need to either be filled in (say, with a mean), or the entire sample discarded. Sensitive information such as personal information may need to be removed.

Data transformation is the process of sampling, reducing, enhancing, or aggregating the dataset to make it more suitable for the algorithm. If the input dataset is small, it may be necessary to enhance it by artificially creating more examples, such as rotating images in an image recognition dataset. If the input dataset has features that the exploration has deemed irrelevant, it would be wise to remove them. If the dataset is more granular than the problem requires, aggregating it to a coarser granularity may help speed up results, such as aggregating city-level data to counties if the problem only requires a prediction per county.

Introducing Machine Learning with Go

Finally, if the input dataset is particularly large, as is the case with many image datasets intended for use by deep learning algorithms, it would be a good idea to start with a smaller sample that will produce fast results so that the viability of the algorithm can be verified before investing in more computing resources.

The sampling process will also divide the input dataset into training and validation subsets. We will explain why this is necessary later, and what proportion of the data to use for both.

Training

The most compute-intensive part of the ML development life cycle is the training process. Training an ML algorithm can take seconds in the simplest case or days when the input dataset is enormous and the algorithm requires many iterations to converge. The latter case is usually observed with deep learning techniques. For example, DeepMinds AlphaGo Zero algorithm took forty days to fully master the game of Go, even though it was proficient after only three[22]. Many algorithms that operate on smaller datasets and problems other than image or sound recognition will not require such a large amount of time or computational resource.

Cloud-based computational resources are getting cheaper and cheaper, so, if an algorithm, especially a deep learning algorithm, is taking too long to train on your PC, you can deploy and train it on a cloud instance for a few dollars. We will cover deployment models in `Chapter 6`, *Deploying Machine Learning Applications*.

While the algorithm is training, particularly if the training phase will take a long time, it is useful to have some real-time measures of how well the training is going, so that it can be interrupted, re-configured, and restarted without waiting for the training to complete. These metrics are typically classified as **loss metrics**, where *loss* refers to the notional error that the algorithm makes either on the training or validation subsets.

Some of the most common loss metrics in prediction problems are as follows:

- **Mean square error** (**MSE**) measures the sum of the squared distance between the output variable and the predicted values.
- **Mean absolute error** (**MAE**) measures the sum of the absolute distance between the output variable and the predicted values.
- **Huber loss** is a combination of the MSE and MAE that is more robust to outliers while remaining a good estimator of both the mean and median loss.

Some of the most common loss metrics in classification problems are as follows:

- **Logarithmic loss** measures the accuracy of the classifier by placing a penalty on false classifications. It is closely related to cross-entropy loss.
- **Focal loss** is a newer `loss` func aimed at preventing false negatives when the input dataset is sparse[23].

Validating/testing

Software engineers are familiar with testing and debugging software source code, but how should ML models be tested? Pieces of algorithms and data input/output routines can be unit tested, but often it is unclear how to ensure that the ML model itself, which presents as a black box, is correct.

The first step to ensuring correctness and sufficient accuracy of an ML model is validation. This means applying the model to predict or classify the validation data subset, and measuring the resulting accuracy against project objectives. Because the training data subset was already seen by the algorithm, it cannot be used to validate correctness, as the model could suffer from poor generalizability (also known as **overfitting**). To take a nonsensical example, imagine an ML model that consists of a hash map that memorizes each input sample and maps it to the corresponding training output sample. The model would have 100% accuracy on a training data subset, which was previously memorized, but very low accuracy on any data subset, and therefore it would not solve the problem it was intended for. Validation tests against this phenomenon.

In addition, it is a good idea to validate model outputs against user acceptance criteria. For example, if building a recommender system for TV series, you may wish to ensure that the recommendations made to children are never rated PG-13 or higher. Rather than trying to encode this into the model, which will have a non-zero failure rate, it is better to push this constraint into the application itself, because the cost of not enforcing it would be too high. Such constraints and business rules should be captured at the start of the project.

Integrating and deploying

The boundary between the ML model and the rest of the application must be defined. For example, will the algorithm expose a `Predict` method that provides a prediction for a given input sample? Will input data processing be required of the caller, or will the algorithm implementation perform it? Once this is defined, it is easier to follow best practice when it comes to testing or mocking the ML model to ensure correctness of the rest of the application. Separation of concerns is important for any application, but for ML applications where one component behaves like a black box, it is essential.

There are a number of possible deployment methods for ML applications. For Go applications, containerization is particularly simple as the compiled binary will have no dependencies (except in some very special cases, such as where bindings to deep learning libraries such as TensorFlow are required). Different cloud vendors also admit serverless deployments and have different **continuous integration/continuous deployment** (**CI/CD**) offerings. Part of the advantage of using a language such as Go is that the application can be deployed very flexibly making use of available tooling for traditional systems applications, and without resorting to a messy polyglot approach.

In `Chapter 6`, *Deploying Machine Learning Applications*, we will take a deep dive into topics such as deployment models, **Platform as a Service** (**PaaS**) versus **Infrastructure as a Service** (**IaaS**), and monitoring and alerting specific to ML applications, leveraging the tools built for the Go language.

Re-validating

It is rare to put a model into production that never requires updating or re-training. A recommender system may need regular re-training as user preferences shift. An image recognition model for car makes and models may need re-training as more models come onto the market. A behavioral forecasting tool that produces one model for each device in an IoT population may need continuous monitoring to ensure that each model still satisfies the desired accuracy criterion, and to retrain those that are not.

The re-validation process is a continuous process where the accuracy of the model is tested and, if it is deemed to have decreased, an automated or manual process is triggered to re-train it, ensuring that the results are always optimal.

Summary

In this chapter, we introduced ML and the different types of ML problems. We argued for Go as a language to develop ML applications. Then, we outlined the ML development life cycle, the process of creating and taking to production an ML application.

In the next chapter, we will explain how to set up a development environment for ML applications and Go.

Further readings

1. https://www.crunchbase.com/hub/machine-learning-companies, retrieved on February 9, 2019.
2. https://www.ft.com/content/133dc9c8-90ac-11e8-9609-3d3b945e78cf. *Machine Learning will be the global engine of growth.*
3. https://news.crunchbase.com/news/venture-funding-ai-machine-learning-levels-off-tech-matures/. Retrieved on February 9, 2019.
4. https://www.economist.com/science-and-technology/2018/02/15/for-artificial-intelligence-to-thrive-it-must-explain-itself. Retrieved on February 9, 2019.
5. https://www.nytimes.com/column/machine-learning. Retrieved on February 9th 2019.
6. See for example *Google Trends for Machine Learning.* https://trends.google.com/trends/explore?date=allamp;geo=USamp;q=machine%20learning.
7. R. Kohavi and F. Provost, *Glossary of Terms, Machine Learning,* vol. 30, no. 2–3, pp. 271–274, 1998. 30, no. 2–3, pp. 271–274, 1998.
8. Turing, Alan (October 1950). *Computing Machinery and Intelligence.* Mind. 59 (236): 433–460. doi:10.1093/mind/LIX.236.433. Retrieved 8 June 2016.016.
9. https://www.forbes.com/sites/bernardmarr/2016/12/06/what-is-the-difference-between-artificial-intelligence-and-machine-learning/. Retrieved on February 9, 2019.
10. https://talks.golang.org/2012/splash.article. Retrieved February 9, 2019.
11. https://talks.golang.org/2012/splash.article. Retrieved February 9,h 2019.
12. https://insights.stackoverflow.com/survey/2018/. Retrieved February 9, 2019.

13. https://github.com/cloudflare. Retrieved February 9, 2019.
14. https://github.com/uber. Retrieved February 9, 2019.
15. https://github.com/dailymotion. Retrieved February 9, 2019.
16. https://github.com/medium. Retrieved February 9, 2019.
17. https://github.com/sjwhitworth/golearn. Retrieved on 10, February 2019.
18. See the MNIST dataset hosted at http://yann.lecun.com/exdb/mnist/. Retrieved February 10, 2019.
19. See https://machinelearningmastery.com/handwritten-digit-recognition-using-convolutional-neural-networks-python-keras/ for an example. Retrieved February 10, 2019.
20. http://cognitivemedium.com/rmnist. Retrieved February 10, 2019.
21. *Regression Models to Predict Corrected Weight, Height and Obesity Prevalence From Self-Reported Data*: data from BRFSS 1999-2007. Int J Obes (Lond). 2010 Nov; 34(11):1655-64. doi: 10.1038/ijo.2010.80. Epub 2010 Apr 13.
22. https://deepmind.com/blog/alphago-zero-learning-scratch/. Retrieved February 10th, 2019.
23. *Focal Loss for Dense Object Detection*. Lin et al. ICCV 2980-2988. Pre-print available at https://arxiv.org/pdf/1708.02002.pdf.

Setting Up the Development Environment

Just like traditional software development, ML application development requires the mastery of specialist boilerplate code and a development environment that allows the developer to proceed at a pace that has the lowest amount of friction and distraction. Software developers typically waste a lot of time with basic setup and data wrangling tasks. Being a productive and professional ML developer requires the ability to quickly prototype solutions; this means expending as little effort as possible on trivial tasks.

In the previous chapter, we outlined the main ML problems and a development process that you can follow to obtain a commercial solution. We also explained the advantages offered by Go as a programming language when creating ML applications.

In this chapter, we will guide you through the steps that are required to set up a development environment for Go that is optimized for ML applications. Specifically, we will cover the following topics:

- How to install Go
- Running Go interactively using Jupyter and gophernotes
- Data wrangling with Gota
- Data visualization with gonum/plot and gophernotes
- Data preprocessing (formatting, cleaning, and sampling)
- Data transformation (normalization and encoding of categorical variables)

 The code examples that accompany this book are optimized for Debian-based Linux distributions. However, they can be adapted for other distributions (for example, by changing `apt` to `yum`) and Windows with Cygwin.

Once you have completed this chapter, you will be able to quickly explore, visualize, and process any dataset for subsequent use by an ML algorithm.

Installing Go

Development environments are personal. Most developers will prefer one code editor or toolset over another. While we recommend the use of interactive tools such as Jupyter via gophernotes, the only prerequisite to running the code examples in this book is a working installation of Go 1.10 or higher. That is, the `go` command should be available and the `GOPATH` environment variable should be set up correctly.

To install Go, download a binary release for your system from https://golang.org/dl/. Then, refer to the one of the following subsections that matches your operating system[2].

 If you only want to use gophernotes to run Go code and you intend to use Docker as the installation method, then you can skip this section and go straight to the *Running Go interactively with gophernotes* section.

Linux, macOS, and FreeBSD

The binary releases are packaged as tarballs. Extract the binaries and add them to your `PATH`. Here's an example:

```
tar -C /usr/local -xzf go$VERSION.$OS-$ARCH.tar.gz && \
    export PATH=$PATH:/usr/local/go/bin
```

To configure your `GOPATH` environment variable, you will need to decide where you will want your Go files, including any personal repositories, to live. One possible location is `$HOME/go`. Once you have decided on this, set the environment variable, for example as follows:

```
export GOPATH=$HOME/go
```

To make this instruction permanent, you will need to add this line to `.bashrc`. For instructions if you're using other shells (such as `.zsh`), please refer to the official Go installation instructions at https://github.com/golang/go/wiki/SettingGOPATH.

> Make sure that your `GOPATH` is not in the same directory as your Go installation, otherwise this can cause issues.

Windows

The binary releases are packaged either as a ZIP file or an MSI installer that automatically configures your environment variables. We recommend using the MSI installer. However, if you do not, then after extracting the contents of the ZIP file to a suitable location (such as `C:\Program Files\Go`), make sure that you add the `subdirectory` bin to your `PATH` environment variable using the control panel.

Once the binaries have been installed to a suitable location, you will need to configure your `GOPATH`. First, decide where you want your Go files, including any personal repositories, to live. One possible location is `C:\go`. Once you have decided, set the `GOPATH` environment variable to the path of this directory.

If you are unsure how to set environment variables, refer to the official Go installation instructions at https://github.com/golang/go/wiki/SettingGOPATH.

> Make sure that your `GOPATH` is not in the same directory as your Go installation, otherwise this can cause issues.

Running Go interactively with gophernotes

Project Jupyter is a not-for-profit organization that was created to develop language-agnostic interactive computing for data science[3]. The result is a mature, well-supported environment to explore, visualize, and process data that can significantly accelerate development by providing immediate feedback and integrations with plotting libraries such as `gonum/plot`.

While its first iteration, called iPython, only supported Python-based handlers (called *kernels*) at first, the latest version of Jupyter has over 50 kernels that support dozens of languages, including three kernels for the Go language[4]. GitHub has support for rendering Jupyter files (called *notebooks*)[5], and there are various specialized hubs for sharing notebooks online, including Google Research Colabs[6], Jupyter's community hub called NBViewer[7], and its enterprise offering, JupyterHub[8]. Notebooks for presentation purposes can be converted into other file formats such as HTML using the nbconvert utility[9].

In this book, we will be using Jupyter together with the gophernotes kernel for Go. The simplest way to get started with gophernotes on Linux and Windows is to use its Docker[10] image.

For alternative installation methods, we recommend checking the README page of the gophernotes GitHub repository at: `https://github.com/gopherdata/gophernotes`.

The steps to begin a new gophernotes-based project are as follows:

1. Create a new directory to hold the project files (this does not need to be in your `GOPATH`).
2. (Optional) Initialize a new git repository by running `git init` in the new directory.
3. Run the following command from the new directory (you may need to prefix it with `sudo`, depending on how you installed Docker):
   `docker run -it -p 8888:8888 -v $(pwd):/usr/share/notebooks gopherdata/gophernotes:latest-ds`
4. In the terminal, there will be a URL ending in `?token=[some combination of letters and numbers]`. Navigate to this URL in a modern web browser. The new directory you created will be mapped to `/usr/share/notebooks`, so navigate to this directory in the tree that presents itself.

On Windows, you may need to modify the preceding command by replacing `$(pwd)` with `%CD%`.

Now that we have learned how to install Go and set up a basic development environment with gophernotes, it's time to learn about data preprocessing.

Example – the most common phrases in positive and negative reviews

In our first code example, we will use the multi-domain sentiment dataset (version 2.0)[11]. This dataset contains Amazon reviews from four different product categories. We will download it, preprocess it, and load it into Gota, a data wrangling library, to find the most common phrases in positive and negative reviews that do not co-occur in both. This is a basic example that involves no ML algorithms, but will serve as a hands-on introduction to Go, gophernotes, and Gota.

> You can find the full code example in the companion repository to this book at https://github.com/PacktPublishing/Machine-Learning-with-Go-Quick-Start-Guide.

Initializing the example directory and downloading the dataset

Following the process we implemented previously, create an empty directory to hold the code files. Before opening gophernotes, download the dataset from `http://www.cs.jhu.edu/~mdredze/datasets/sentiment/processed_acl.tar.gz` and extract it to `datasets/words`. On most Linux distributions, you can do this with the following script:

```
mkdir -p datasets/words && \
wget http://www.cs.jhu.edu/~mdredze/datasets/sentiment/processed_acl.tar.gz -O datasets/words-temp.tar.gz && \
tar xzvf datasets/words-temp.tar.gz -C datasets/words && \
rm datasets/words-temp.tar.gz
```

Now, start gophernotes and navigate the tree to `/usr/share/notebooks`. Create a new Notebook by clicking on **New** | **Go**. You will see a blank Jupyter Notebook:

Setting Up the Development Environment

Input cells in Jupyter are marked with the `In` label. When you run the code in an input cell (*Shift + Enter*), a new output cell will be created with the result, marked as `Out`. Each cell is numbered with its execution order. For example, the `In [1]` cell is the first cell you ran within a given session.

Try running some Go statements, like the following snippet:

```
a := 1
import "fmt"
fmt.Println("Hello, world")
a
```

In particular, note that the `a` variable is displayed in the output cell, even though there was no call to `fmt.Println()`.

 All the imports, variables, and funcs you define within a session remain in memory, even if you delete the input cells. To clear the current scope, go to **Kernel | Restart**.

Loading the dataset files

One of the basic tasks of data processing is to read the input file and load its contents. A simple way to do this is to use the `io/ioutil` utility func `ReadFile`. Unlike in a `.go` file, where you would need to place this code inside your `main` func, with gophernotes, you can run the following code without declaring any func at all:

```
import "io/ioutil"

const kitchenReviews = "../datasets/words/processed_acl/kitchen"

positives, err := ioutil.ReadFile(kitchenReviews + "/positive.review")
negatives, err2 := ioutil.ReadFile(kitchenReviews + "/negative.review")
if err != nil || err2 != nil {
  fmt.Println("Error(s)", err, err2)
}
```

The preceding code will load the contents of reviews of kitchen products with positive sentiments into a byte slice called `positives` and the ones with negative sentiments into the byte slice called `negatives`. If you have correctly downloaded the datasets and you run this code, it should not output anything because there are no errors. If any errors appear, check that the dataset files have been extracted to the correct folder.

[26]

If you have opened the `positive.review` or `negative.review` file in a text editor, you may have noticed that they are formatted as a space or newline separated list of pairs, that is, `phrase:frequency`. For example, the start of the positive review is as follows:

```
them_it:1 hovering:1 and_occasional:1 cousin_the:2 fictional_baudelaire:1
their_struggles:1
```

In the next subsection, we will parse these pairs into a Go struct.

Parsing contents into a Struct

We will use the `strings` package to parse the contents of the data files into slices of pairs. Each item in the slice of strings will contain a single pair, such as `them_it:1`. We will then further split this pair by the colon symbol and use the `strconv` package to parse the integer frequency into an `int`. Each `Pair` will be of the following type:

```go
type Pair struct {
  Phrase string
  Frequency int
}
```

We will do this as follows:

1. First, observe that the separation between the pairs can be either a new line (\n) or a space. We will use the `strings.Fields` func of the strings package, which will split the string by any consecutive whitespace characters:

   ```go
   pairsPositive := strings.Fields(string(positives))
   pairsNegative := strings.Fields(string(negatives))
   ```

2. Now, we will iterate each pair, splitting by the colon separator and using the `strconv` package to parse the frequency to an integer:

   ```go
   // pairsAndFilters returns a slice of Pair, split by : to obtain the phrase and frequency,
   // as well as a map of the phrases that can be used as a lookup table later.
   func pairsAndFilters(splitPairs []string) ([]Pair, map[string]bool) {
     var (
       pairs []Pair
       m map[string]bool
     )
     m = make(map[string]bool)
     for _, pair := range splitPairs {
   ```

```
      p := strings.Split(pair, ":")
      phrase := p[0]
      m[phrase] = true
      if len(p) < 2 {
        continue
      }
      freq, err := strconv.Atoi(p[1])
      if err != nil {
        continue
      }
      pairs = append(pairs, Pair{
        Phrase: phrase,
        Frequency: freq,
      })
    }
    return pairs, m
}
```

3. We will also return a map of phrases so that we can later exclude phrases that are in the intersection between positive and negative reviews. The reason for doing this is that words that are common to both positive and negative reviews are less likely to be indicative of the positive or negative sentiment. This is done with the following function:

```
// exclude returns a slice of Pair that does not contain the
phrases in the exclusion map
func exclude(pairs []Pair, exclusions map[string]bool) []Pair {
  var ret []Pair
  for i := range pairs {
    if !exclusions[pairs[i].Phrase] {
      ret = append(ret, pairs[i])
    }
  }
  return ret
}
```

4. Finally, we will apply this to our slices of pairs:

```
parsedPositives, posPhrases := pairsAndFilters(pairsPositive)
parsedNegatives, negPhrases := pairsAndFilters(pairsNegative)
parsedPositives = exclude(parsedPositives, negPhrases)
parsedNegatives = exclude(parsedNegatives, posPhrases)
```

The next step is to load the parsed pairs into Gota, the data wrangling library for Go.

Loading the data into a Gota dataframe

The Gota library contains implementation of dataframes, series, and some general data wrangling algorithms[12]. The concept of a dataframe is integral to a number of popular data science libraries and languages such as Python's pandas, R, and Julia. In a nutshell, a **dataframe** is a list of lists (called a **column** or **series**) that each have the same length. Every list has a name—the column name or series name, depending on the nomenclature favored by the library. This abstraction mimics a database table and makes an easy fundamental building block for mathematical and statistical tools.

The Gota library has two packages: the `dataframe` and the `series` packages. The series package contains functions and structures to represent individual lists, whereas the `dataframe` package deals with the entire dataframe—that is, the table—as a whole. A Go developer may wish to use Gota to quickly sort, filter, aggregate, or perform relational operations, such as inner joins between two tables, saving on boilerplate code such as implementing a `sort` interface[13].

There are several ways to create a new dataframe with Gota:

- `dataframe.New(se ...series.Series)`: Accepts a slice of series (which can be created via the `series.New` func).
- `dataframe.LoadRecords(records [][]string, options ...LoadOption)`: Accepts a slice of slices. The first slice will be a slice of strings representing the column names.
- `dataframe.LoadStructs(i interface{}, options ...LoadOption)`: Accepts a slice of structs. Gota will use reflection to determine the column names based on the struct field names.
- `dataframe.LoadMaps(maps []map[string][]interface{})`: Accepts a slice of maps of column names to slices.
- `dataframe.LoadMatrix(mat Matrix)`: Accepts a slice that is compatible with the mat64 matrix interface.

In our case, because we have parsed the data into structs, we will use the `LoadStructs` function, making one dataframe for positive reviews and one for negative reviews:

```
dfPos := dataframe.LoadStructs(parsedPositives)
dfNeg := dataframe.LoadStructs(parsedNegatives)
```

Setting Up the Development Environment

> **TIP**
> If you want to inspect the content of a dataframe, that is, `df`, just use `fmt.Println(df)`. This will show you the first 10 rows of the dataframe, along with its column names and some useful metadata, such as the total number of rows.

Finding the most common phrases

Now that the data has been parsed, the co-occurring phrases have been filtered out, and the resulting phrase/frequency pairs have been loaded into dataframes, all that is remaining is to find the most common phrases for the positive and negative reviews and display them. One way of doing this without dataframes would be to create a `type ByFrequency []Pair` type that implements the `sort` interface, and then compose `sort.Reverse` and `sort.Sort` to order positive pairs and negative pairs by descending frequency. However, by using Gota, we can achieve this with one line per dataframe:

```
dfPos = dfPos.Arrange(dataframe.RevSort("Frequency"))
dfNeg = dfNeg.Arrange(dataframe.RevSort("Frequency"))
```

Printing the dataframes now gives the top 10 most common phrases for positive and negative reviews of kitchen items, respectively. For positive reviews, we have the following output:

```
[46383x2] DataFrame

    Phrase        Frequency

 0: tic-tac-toe   10
 1: wusthoff      7
 2: emperor       7
 3: shot_glasses  6
 4: pulp          6
 5: games         6
 6: sentry        6
 7: gravel        6
 8: the_emperor   5
```

```
9: aebleskivers    5

   ...             ...

   <string>        <int>
```

For negative reviews, we have the following output:

```
[45760x2] DataFrame

   Phrase           Frequency
0: seeds            9

1: perculator       7

2: probes           7

3: cork             7

4: coffee_tank      5

5: brookstone       5

6: convection_oven  5

7: black_goo        5

8: waring_pro       5

9: packs            5

   ...              ...

   <string>         <int>
```

This completes this example. In the following section, we will cover the other transformation and processing features of Gota in more detail.

Example – exploring body mass index data with gonum/plot

In the previous section, we introduced gophernotes and Gota. In this section, we will explore a dataset containing 500 samples of gender, height, and BMI index. We will do this using the `gonum/plot` library. This library, which was originally a fork of the 2012 Plotinum library[15], contains several packages that make creating data visualizations in Go much easier[16]:

- The `plot` package contains a layout and formatting interface.
- The `plotter` package abstracts the layout and formatting for common plot types, such as bar charts, scatter plots, and so on.
- The `plotutil` package contains utility funcs for common plot types.
- The `vg` package exposes an API for vector graphics and is particularly useful when exporting plots to other software. We will not be covering this package.

Installing gonum and gonum/plot

Regardless of whether you are using the Docker image to run gophernotes as suggested previously or a different method, you will need to use `gonum/plot`. To do this, run the `go get gonum.org/v1/plot/...` command. If you do not have the `gonum` library installed, and you are not using the gophernotes Docker image, you will need to install this separately using the `go get github.com/gonum/...` command.

> **TIP**
> To open a terminal from Jupyter, open up the web UI to the tree view (the default view) and then click on **New** | **Terminal**.

Note that, despite their names, gonum and gonum/plot are not part of the same repository, so you need to install both separately.

Loading the data

If you have cloned the project repository, it will already contain the 500-person BMI dataset in the `datasets/bmi` folder. You can also download the dataset yourself from Kaggle[14]. The dataset is a single CSV file with the following first few rows:

```
Gender,Height,Weight,Index
Male,174,96,4
Male,189,87,2
Female,185,110,4
Female,195,104,3
Male,149,61,3
...
```

Like in the previous section, we will use `io/ioutil` to read the file into a byte slice, but this time, we will take advantage of Gota's ReadCSV method (which takes an `io.Reader` as an argument) to directly load the data into a dataframe with no preprocessing:

```
b, err := ioutil.ReadFile(path)
if err != nil {
  fmt.Println("Error!", err)
}
df := dataframe.ReadCSV(bytes.NewReader(b))
```

Inspect the dataframe to make sure that the data has been loaded correctly:

```
[500x4] DataFrame

    Gender  Height Weight Index
 0: Male    174    96     4

 1: Male    189    87     2

 2: Female  185    110    4

 3: Female  195    104    3

 4: Male    149    61     3

 5: Male    189    104    3

 6: Male    147    92     5

 7: Male    154    111    5

 8: Male    174    90     3
```

```
9:  Female   169     103     4

    ...      ...     ...     ...

    <string> <int>   <int>   <int>
```

Note that the data types of the series have been inferred automatically.

Understanding the distributions of the data series

A good way to understand each series is to plot a histogram. This will give you an impression of how each series is distributed. Using gonum/plot, we will plot histograms for each series. However, before we plot anything, we can quickly access some summary statistics via Gota to gain a rudimentary understanding of the dataset:

```
fmt.Println("Minimum", df.Col("Height").Min())
fmt.Println("Maximum", df.Col("Height").Max())
fmt.Println("Mean", df.Col("Height").Mean())
fmt.Println("Median", df.Col("Height").Quantile(0.5))
```

This tells us that the heights of the sampled individuals lie between 140 cm and 199 cm, that their mean and median are 169 cm and 170 cm, respectively, and the fact that the mean and the median are so close suggests low skewness—that is, a symmetric distribution.

An even quicker way to achieve this for all columns simultaneously is to use the dataframe.Describe function. This produces another dataframe that contains summary statistics of each column:

```
[7x5] DataFrame

    column    Gender    Height       Weight       Index
0:  mean      -         169.944000   106.000000   3.748000

1:  stddev    -         16.375261    32.382607    1.355053

2:  min       Female    140.000000   50.000000    0.000000

3:  25%       -         156.000000   80.000000    3.000000

4:  50%       -         170.000000   106.000000   4.000000

5:  75%       -         184.000000   136.000000   5.000000
```

```
6: max     Male       199.000000 160.000000 5.000000

      <string> <string> <float>    <float>    <float>
```

Now, we will visualize the distributions using histograms. First, we will need to convert a column of a Gota dataframe into a plot-friendly `plotter.Values` slice. This can be accomplished with the following utility function:

```
// SeriesToPlotValues takes a column of a Dataframe and converts it to a
gonum/plot/plotter.Values slice.
// Panics if the column does not exist.
func SeriesToPlotValues(df dataframe.DataFrame, col string) plotter.Values
{
  rows, _ := df.Dims()
  v := make(plotter.Values, rows)
  s := df.Col(col)
  for i := 0; i < rows; i++ {
    v[i] = s.Elem(i).Float()
  }
  return v
}
```

The `dataframe.Col` func extracts just the required column from the given dataframe—in our case, a single column. You can also use `dataframe.Select`, which takes a slice of strings of column names to return a dataframe containing only the required columns. This can be useful for discarding unnecessary data.

Now, we can use gonum/plot to create a JPEG image of a histogram of a given column with a chosen title:

```
// HistogramData returns a byte slice of JPEG data for a histogram of the
column with name col in the dataframe df.
func HistogramData(v plotter.Values, title string) []byte {
  // Make a plot and set its title.
  p, err := plot.New()
  if err != nil {
    panic(err)
  }
  p.Title.Text = title
  h, err := plotter.NewHist(v, 10)
  if err != nil {
    panic(err)
  }
  //h.Normalize(1) // Uncomment to normalize the area under the histogram to 1
  p.Add(h)
  w, err := p.WriterTo(5*vg.Inch, 4*vg.Inch, "jpg")
```

```
    if err != nil {
      panic(err)
    }
    var b bytes.Buffer
    writer := bufio.NewWriter(&b)
    w.WriteTo(writer)
    return b.Bytes()
}
```

To display the resulting plot using gophernotes, use the appropriate method of the display object. In this case, we are producing a JPEG image, so calling `display.JPEG` with the byte slice that was produced by the preceding code will display the plot in the output cell. The full code input cell would be as follows:

```
Display.JPEG(HistogramData(SeriesToPlotValues(df, "Age"), "Age Histogram"))
```

In general, the steps to create a new plot from one of gonum's built-in plotters are as follows:

1. Create a new plot with `plot.New()` – this is like a canvas that the plot will live on.
2. Set any plot attributes, such as its title.
3. Create a new plotter based on one of the available types (`BarChart`, `BoxPlot`, `ColorBar`, `Contour`, `HeatMap`, `Histogram`, `Line`, `QuartPlot`, `Sankey`, or `Scatter`).
4. Set any plotter attributes and add the plotter to the plot by calling its `Add` method.
5. If you wish to display the plot via gophernotes, use the `WriterTo` method and a byte buffer to output the plot data as a slice of bytes that can be passed to the built-in display object. Otherwise, use `p.Save` to save the image to a file.

> If, instead of displaying the image in gophernotes, you wish to save it, you can do this with the plot's `Save` method. For example, `p.Save(5*vg.Inch, 4*vg.Inch, title + ".png")` will save the plot to a 5" x 4" PNG file.

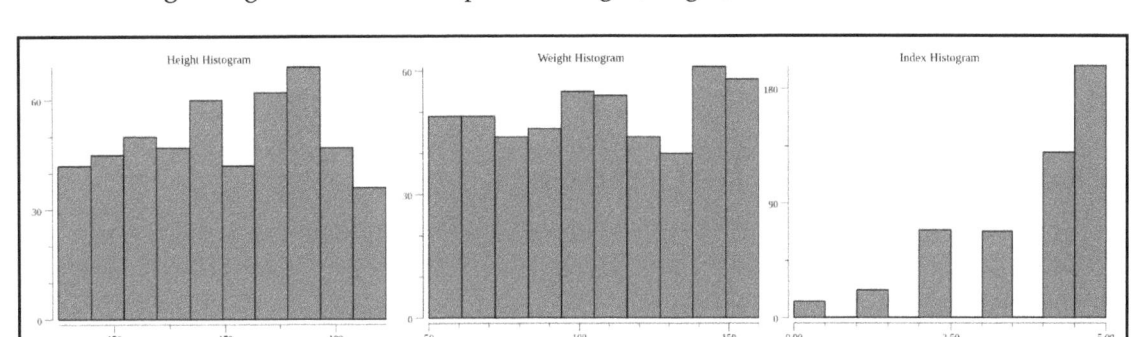

The resulting histograms for the 500-person weight/height/BMI dataset are as follows:

In the following example, we will not just load and visualize data, but also transform it to make it more suitable for use with an ML algorithm.

Example – preprocessing data with Gota

The quality and speed of the ML algorithm training process depends on the quality of the input data. While many algorithms are robust to irrelevant columns and data that is not normalized, some are not. For example, many models requires data inputs to be normalized to lie between 0 and 1. In this section, we will look at some quick and easy ways to preprocess data with Gota. For these examples, we will be using a dataset containing 1,035 records of the height (inch) and weight (lbs) of major league baseball players[17]. The dataset, as described on the UCLA website, consists of the following features:

- Name: Player name
- Team: The baseball team that the player was a member of
- Position: The player's position
- Height (inches): Player height
- Weight (pounds): Player weight in pounds
- Age: Player age at the time of recording

For the purposes of this exercise, we will preprocess the data in the following manner:

- Remove the name and team column
- Convert the height and weight columns into the float type
- Filter out players with a weight greater than or equal to 260 pounds

Setting Up the Development Environment

- Normalize the height and weight columns
- Divide the data into training and validation subsets with approximately 70% of rows in the training subset and 30% in the validation subset

Loading the data into Gota

The dataset is supplied as an HTML table on the UCLA website[17]. In the companion repository to this book, you will find a CSV version. To quickly convert the HTML table yourself into CSV format without needing to write any code, first highlight the table and copy and paste this into a spreadsheet program such as Microsoft Excel. Then, save the spreadsheet as a CSV file. Open this file in a text editor to ensure there are no artefacts or extraneous rows in the file.

Loading the dataset is done using the `dataframe.ReadCSV` method. Inspecting the dataframe produces the following output:

```
[1034x6] DataFrame

    Name              Team    Position         Height(inches)  Weight(pounds)
...
 0: Adam_Donachie    BAL     Catcher          74              180
...
 1: Paul_Bako        BAL     Catcher          74              215
...
 2: Ramon_Hernandez  BAL     Catcher          72              210
...
 3: Kevin_Millar     BAL     First_Baseman    72              210
...
 4: Chris_Gomez      BAL     First_Baseman    73              188
...
 5: Brian_Roberts    BAL     Second_Baseman   69              176
...
 6: Miguel_Tejada    BAL     Shortstop        69              209
...
 7: Melvin_Mora      BAL     Third_Baseman    71              200
...
```

```
    8: Aubrey_Huff      BAL         Third_Baseman    76            231
...

    9: Adam_Stern       BAL         Outfielder       71            180
...

        ...             ...         ...              ...           ...
...

    <string>         <string>   <string>         <int>         <int>
...

Not Showing: Age <float>
```

Removing and renaming columns

For this exercise, we have decided that we do not need the `Name` or the `Team` columns. We can use the dataframe's `Select` method to specify a slice of strings of column names that we wish to keep:

```
df = df.Select([]string{"Position", "Height(inches)", "Weight(pounds)", "Age"})
```

While we are at it, the `Height` and `Weight` columns should be renamed to remove the units from the column names. This can be achieved with the `Rename` method:

```
df = df.Rename("Height", "Height(inches)")
df = df.Rename("Weight", "Weight(pounds)")
```

The resulting dataset is as follows:

```
[1034x4] DataFrame

    Position         Height Weight Age

 0: Catcher          74     180    22.990000

 1: Catcher          74     215    34.690000

 2: Catcher          72     210    30.780000

 3: First_Baseman    72     210    35.430000

 4: First_Baseman    73     188    35.710000

 5: Second_Baseman   69     176    29.390000
```

```
6:  Shortstop         69    209   30.770000

7:  Third_Baseman     71    200   35.070000

8:  Third_Baseman     76    231   30.190000

9:  Outfielder        71    180   27.050000

    ...               ...   ...   ...

    <string>          <int> <int> <float>
```

Converting a column into a different type

Our dataframe now has the correct columns with more concise names. However, the height and weight columns are of the `int` type, whereas we need them to be of the `float` type so that we can correctly normalize their values. The easiest way to do this is to add this as a `LoadOption` when first loading the data into a dataframe. Namely, `func WithTypes(coltypes map[string]series.Type) LoadOption` accepts a map of column names to series types, and we can use this to perform the conversion at load time.

However, suppose that we have not done this. In that case, we convert the column type by replacing the column with a new series that has the correct type. To generate this series, we can use the `series.New` method, together with `df.Col` to isolate the column of interest. For example, to produce a series of floats from the current height series, we can use the following code:

```
heightFloat := series.New(df.Col("Height"), series.Float, "Height")
```

To replace the column, we can use the `Mutate` method:

```
df.Mutate(heightFloat)
```

Doing this for both the `Height` and the `Weight` columns now produces the following output:

```
[1034x4] DataFrame

    Position       Height    Weight     Age
0:  Catcher        74.00000  180.00000  22.990000

1:  Catcher        74.00000  215.00000  34.690000

2:  Catcher        72.00000  210.00000  30.780000
```

```
3: First_Baseman    72.00000    210.00000   35.430000

4: First_Baseman    73.00000    188.00000   35.710000

5: Second_Baseman  69.00000    176.00000   29.390000

6: Shortstop        69.00000    209.00000   30.770000

7: Third_Baseman   71.00000    200.00000   35.070000

8: Third_Baseman   76.00000    231.00000   30.190000

9: Outfielder       71.00000    180.00000   27.050000

   ...              ...         ...         ...

   <string>         <float>     <float>     <float>
```

Filtering out unwanted data

Suppose that, after exploring the data, we do not wish to keep samples where the player weight is greater than or equal to 260 pounds. This could be because there are not enough samples of heavier players, and so any analysis would not be representative of the player population as a whole. Such players could be called **outliers** in regards to the current dataset.

> You can find the reference (Godocs) for the Gota library at https://godoc.org/github.com/kniren/gota.

Gota dataframes can be filtered using the `Filter` func. This accepts a `dataframe.F` struct, which consists of the target column, a comparator, and a value, such as `{"Column", series.Eq, 1}`, which would match only rows where `Column` was equal to 1. The available comparators are as follows:

- `series.Eq`: Keeps only rows that are equal to the given value
- `series.Neq`: Keeps only rows that are not equal to the given value
- `series.Greater`: Keeps only rows that are greater than the given value

- `series.GreaterEq`: Keeps only rows that are greater than or equal to the given value
- `series.Less`: Keeps only rows that are less than the given value
- `series.LessEq`: Keeps only rows that are less than or equal to the given value

> **TIP**
> The `series.Comparator` type is an alias for a string. These strings are the same as the ones that are used in the Go language itself. For example, `series.Neq` is equivalent to `"!="`.

For this exercise, we will apply the series. We will use the `less` filter in order to remove rows where the weight is greater than or equal to 260 pounds:

```
df = df.Filter(dataframe.F{"Weight", "<", 260})
```

Normalizing the Height, Weight, and Age columns

Data normalization, also known as feature scaling, is the process of transforming a group of independent variables to map them onto the same range. There are several methods to achieve this:

- **Rescaling (min/max normalization)**: This will linearly map the variable range onto the [0,1] range, where the minimum value of the series will map to 0 and its maximum will map to 1. This is achieved by applying the following formula:

$$x' = \frac{x - x_{min}}{x_{max} - x_{min}}$$

- **Mean normalization**: This will map the variable range if we apply the following formula:

$$x' = \frac{x - \bar{x}}{x_{max} - x_{min}}$$

- **Standardization (z-score normalization)**: This very common method of normalization for ML applications uses the mean and standard deviation to transform the series of values into their z-scores, that is, how many standard deviations from the mean the data point lies. This is done by computing the mean and standard deviation of the series and then applying the following formula:

$$x' = \frac{x - \bar{x}}{\sigma}$$

> Note that this is not guaranteed to map the variable onto a closed range.

Rescaling can be implemented with the following utility func:

```
// rescale maps the given column values onto the range [0,1]
func rescale(df dataframe.DataFrame, col string) dataframe.DataFrame {
    s := df.Col(col)
    min := s.Min()
    max := s.Max()
    v := make([]float64, s.Len(), s.Len())
    for i := 0; i < s.Len(); i++ {
        v[i] = (s.Elem(i).Float() - min) / (max - min)
    }
    rs := series.Floats(v)
    rs.Name = col
    return df.Mutate(rs)
}
```

Mean normalization can be implemented with the following utility function:

```
// meanNormalise maps the given column values onto the range [-1,1] by
subtracting mean and dividing by max - min
func meanNormalise(df dataframe.DataFrame, col string) dataframe.DataFrame
{
    s := df.Col(col)
    min := s.Min()
    max := s.Max()
    mean := s.Mean()
    v := make([]float64, s.Len(), s.Len())
    for i := 0; i < s.Len(); i++ {
        v[i] = (s.Elem(i).Float() - mean) / (max - min)
    }
    rs := series.Floats(v)
```

Setting Up the Development Environment

```
    rs.Name = col
    return df.Mutate(rs)
}
```

Standardization can be implemented with the following utility func:

```
// meanNormalise maps the given column values onto the range [-1,1] by
subtracting mean and dividing by max - min
func standardise(df dataframe.DataFrame, col string) dataframe.DataFrame {
  s := df.Col(col)
  std := s.StdDev()
  mean := s.Mean()
  v := make([]float64, s.Len(), s.Len())
  for i := 0; i < s.Len(); i++ {
    v[i] = (s.Elem(i).Float() - mean) / std
  }
  rs := series.Floats(v)
  rs.Name = col
  return df.Mutate(rs)
}
```

For this example, we will apply rescaling to the `Height` and `Weight` columns with the following code:

```
df = rescale(df, "Height")
df = rescale(df, "Weight")
```

The result is as follows. Note that the values of the `Height` and `Weight` columns now lie between 0 and 1, as intended:

```
[1034x4] DataFrame

    Position         Height    Weight    Age

 0: Catcher          0.437500  0.214286  22.990000

 1: Catcher          0.437500  0.464286  34.690000

 2: Catcher          0.312500  0.428571  30.780000

 3: First_Baseman    0.312500  0.428571  35.430000

 4: First_Baseman    0.375000  0.271429  35.710000

 5: Second_Baseman   0.125000  0.185714  29.390000

 6: Shortstop        0.125000  0.421429  30.770000
```

```
7: Third_Baseman   0.250000 0.357143 35.070000

8: Third_Baseman   0.562500 0.578571 30.190000

9: Outfielder      0.250000 0.214286 27.050000

   ...             ...      ...      ...

   <string>        <float>  <float>  <float>
```

Sampling to obtain training/validation subsets

When training an ML algorithm, it is useful to reserve a portion of the dataset for validation. This is used to test the generalization of the model to previously unseen data and thus to ensure its usefulness when presented with real-life data that isn't part of the training set. Without the validation step, it is not possible to say whether a model will have good predictive power.

While there are no accepted conventions regarding how much of the dataset to reserve for validation, a fraction between 10% and 30% is common. Research that has been conducted into how much of the dataset to reserve for validation concluded that the more adjustable parameters a model has, the less the fraction of the data needs to be reserved for validation[18]. For this exercise, we will divide our MLB dataset into two subsets: a training subset containing approximately 70% of samples, and a validation subset containing 30% of samples. There are two ways of doing this:

- Select the first 70% of rows to form part of the training subset and the second 30% to form part of the validation subset
- Select a random 70% of samples to form part of the training subset and use the remainder for the validation subset

In general, it is better to avoid deterministic sampling to ensure that both subsets are representative of the overall population. To implement random sampling, we will use the `math/rand` package to produce random indices and combine this with Gota's `dataframe.Subset` method. The first step is to generate a random permutation of the indices of the dataframe:

```
rand.Perm(df.Nrow())
```

Setting Up the Development Environment

Now, we will take the first 70% of this slice for training and the remaining elements for validation, resulting in the following utility:

```
// split splits the dataframe into training and validation subsets.
valFraction (0 <= valFraction <= 1) of the samples
// are reserved for validation and the rest are for training.
func Split(df dataframe.DataFrame, valFraction float64) (training
dataframe.DataFrame, validation dataframe.DataFrame) {
  perm := rand.Perm(df.Nrow())
  cutoff := int(valFraction * float64(len(perm)))
  training = df.Subset(perm[:cutoff])
  validation = df.Subset(perm[cutoff:len(perm)])
  return training, validation
}
```

Applying this to our dataframe with `split(df, 0.7)` produces the following output. The first dataframe is the training subset, while the second is the validation subset:

```
[723x4] DataFrame

    Position           Height   Weight   Age
 0: Relief_Pitcher     0.500000 0.285714 25.640000

 1: Starting_Pitcher   0.500000 0.500000 33.410000

 2: Second_Baseman     0.375000 0.235714 28.200000

 3: Relief_Pitcher     0.562500 0.392857 33.310000

 4: Outfielder         0.187500 0.250000 27.450000

 5: Relief_Pitcher     0.500000 0.042857 27.320000

 6: Relief_Pitcher     0.562500 0.428571 40.970000

 7: Second_Baseman     0.250000 0.357143 33.150000

 8: Outfielder         0.312500 0.071429 25.180000

 9: Relief_Pitcher     0.562500 0.321429 29.990000

    ...                ...      ...      ...

    <string>           <float>  <float>  <float>

[310x4] DataFrame

    Position           Height   Weight   Age
```

[46]

```
0: Relief_Pitcher    0.375000 0.285714 25.080000

1: Relief_Pitcher    0.437500 0.285714 28.310000

2: Outfielder        0.437500 0.357143 34.140000

3: Shortstop         0.187500 0.285714 25.080000

4: Starting_Pitcher  0.500000 0.428571 32.550000

5: Outfielder        0.250000 0.250000 30.550000

6: Starting_Pitcher  0.500000 0.357143 28.480000

7: Third_Baseman     0.250000 0.285714 30.960000

8: Catcher           0.250000 0.421429 30.670000

9: Third_Baseman     0.500000 0.428571 25.480000

   ...               ...      ...      ...

   <string>          <float>  <float>  <float>
```

Encoding data with categorical variables

In the preceding dataframe, the `Position` column is a string. Suppose we want an ML algorithm to use this input, because, say, we are attempting to predict the weight of the player and players in certain positions tend to have different body composition. In this case, we need to **encode** the string to a numerical value that can be used by the algorithm.

The naive solution is to determine the set of all player positions and assign an increasing integer to each member of the set. For example, we might end up with the `{Relief_Pitcher, Starting_Pitcher, Shortstop, Outfielder,...}` set, whereupon we would assign 0 to `Relief_Pitcher`, 1 to `Starting_Pitcher`, 2 to `Shortstop`, and so on. However, the flaw of this approach is in how the numbers are assigned, because it gives importance to the order of the categories where none exist. Suppose that a step of the ML algorithm computes a mean across categories. Therefore, it might conclude that `Starting_Pitcher` is the mean of `Relief_Pitcher` and `Shortstop`! Other types of algorithms might infer correlations where none exist.

Setting Up the Development Environment

To solve this issue, we can use **one-hot encoding**. This type of encoding will split a categorical column with N possible values into N columns. Each of the columns, which correspond to one of the categories, will have the value 1, where that input belongs to the given column, and 0 otherwise. This also allows for the scenario where an input sample may belong to multiple categories.

The steps to generate a one-hot encoding for a given column with Gota are as follows:

1. Enumerate the unique values of the categorical column
2. Create a new series for each unique value, mapping each row to 1 if it belongs to this category and 0 otherwise
3. Mutate the original dataframe by adding the series created in *step 2* and removing the original column

Enumerating the unique values can be done easily using a map:

```
func UniqueValues(df dataframe.DataFrame, col string) []string {
  var ret []string
  m := make(map[string]bool)
  for _, val := range df.Col(col).Records() {
    m[val] = true
  }
  for key := range m {
    ret = append(ret, key)
  }
  return ret
}
```

Note that this makes use of the `series.Records` method to return the values of a given column as a slice of strings. Also, note that the order in which the values are returned will not necessarily be the same every time. Running this func on our dataframe with `UniqueValues(df, "Position")` yields the following unique values:

```
[Shortstop Outfielder Starting_Pitcher Relief_Pitcher Second_Baseman
First_Baseman Third_Baseman Designated_Hitter Catcher]
```

The second step is to iterate over the dataframe, creating new series as we go along:

```
func OneHotSeries(df dataframe.DataFrame, col string, vals []string)
[]series.Series {
  m := make(map[string]int)
  s := make([]series.Series, len(vals), len(vals))
  //cache the mapping for performance reasons
  for i := range vals {
    m[vals[i]] = i
  }
```

```
    for i := range s {
      vals := make([]int, df.Col(col).Len(), df.Col(col).Len())
      for j, val := range df.Col(col).Records() {
        if i == m[val] {
          vals[j] = 1
        }
      }
      s[i] = series.Ints(vals)
    }
    for i := range vals {
      s[i].Name = vals[i]
    }
    return s
}
```

This func will return one series for each unique value of the categorical variable. These series will have the names of the categories. In our case, we can call it with `OneHotSeries(df, "Position", UniqueValues(df, "Position"))`. Now, we will mutate our original dataframe and drop the `Position` column:

```
ohSeries := OneHotSeries(df, "Position", UniqueValues(df, "Position"))
for i := range ohSeries {
  df = df.Mutate(ohSeries[i])
}
```

Printing `df` yields the following result:

```
[1034x13] DataFrame

    Position         Height   Weight   Age        Shortstop Catcher ...

 0: Catcher          0.437500 0.214286 22.990000  0         1       ...

 1: Catcher          0.437500 0.464286 34.690000  0         1       ...

 2: Catcher          0.312500 0.428571 30.780000  0         1       ...

 3: First_Baseman    0.312500 0.428571 35.430000  0         0       ...

 4: First_Baseman    0.375000 0.271429 35.710000  0         0       ...

 5: Second_Baseman   0.125000 0.185714 29.390000  0         0       ...

 6: Shortstop        0.125000 0.421429 30.770000  1         0       ...

 7: Third_Baseman    0.250000 0.357143 35.070000  0         0       ...

 8: Third_Baseman    0.562500 0.578571 30.190000  0         0       ...
```

```
9: Outfielder     0.250000 0.214286 27.050000 0         0         ...

   ...            ...       ...       ...       ...       ...       ...

   <string>       <float>   <float>   <float>   <int>     <int>     ...

Not Showing: Second_Baseman <int>, Outfielder <int>, Designated_Hitter
<int>,

Starting_Pitcher <int>, Relief_Pitcher <int>, First_Baseman <int>,
Third_Baseman <int>
```

To conclude, just drop the `Position` column using `df = df.Drop("Position")`.

Summary

In this chapter, we covered how to set up a development environment for Go that is optimized for ML applications. We explained how to install an interactive environment, Jupyter, to accelerate data exploration and visualization using libraries such as Gota and gonum/plot.

We also introduced some basic data processing steps, such as filtering outliers, removing unnecessary columns, and normalization. Finally, we covered sampling. This chapter took the first few steps in the ML life cycle: data acquisition, exploration, and preparation. Now that you have read this chapter, you have learned how to load data into a Gota dataframe, how to use the dataframe and series packages to process and prepare the data into a format that is required by your chosen algorithm, and how to visualize it with gonum's plot package. You have also learned about different ways of normalizing the data, which is an important step for improving the accuracy and speed of many ML algorithms.

In the next chapter, we will introduce supervised learning algorithms and exemplify how to choose an ML algorithm, train it, and validate its predictive power on previously unseen data.

Further readings

1. *Software Development Waste*. Todd Sedano and Paul Ralph. ICSE '17 Proceedings of the 39th International Conference on Software Engineering. Pages 130-140.
2. See the official Go installation instructions at `https://golang.org/doc/install`. Retrieved February 19th, 2019.
3. `https://jupyter.org/about`. Retrieved February 19th, 2019.
4. `https://github.com/jupyter/jupyter/wiki/Jupyter-kernels`. Retrieved February 19th, 2019.
5. For further instructions, see `https://help.github.com/articles/working-with-jupyter-notebook-files-on-github/`. Retrieved February 19th, 2019.
6. `https://colab.research.google.com`. Retrieved February 19th, 2019.
7. `https://nbviewer.jupyter.org/`. Retrieved February 19th, 2019.
8. `https://jupyter.org/hub`. Retrieved February 19th, 2019.
9. `https://github.com/jupyter/nbconvert`. Retrieved February 19th, 2019.
10. For Docker installation instructions, see `https://docs.docker.com/install/` for Linux and `https://docs.docker.com/docker-for-windows/install/` for Windows. Retrieved February 19th, 2019.
11. John Blitzer, Mark Dredze, Fernando Pereira. Biographies, Bollywood, *Boomboxes and Blenders: Domain Adaptation for Sentiment Classification*. Association of Computational Linguistics (ACL), 2007.
12. `https://github.com/go-gota/gota`. Retrieved February 19th, 2019.
13. `https://godoc.org/sort#Interface`. Retrieved February 19th, 2019.
14. `https://www.kaggle.com/yersever/500-person-gender-height-weight-bodymassindex/version/2`. Retrieved February 20th, 2019.
15. `https://code.google.com/archive/p/plotinum/`. Retrieved February 20th, 2019.
16. `https://github.com/gonum/plot`. Retrieved February 20th, 2019.
17. `http://wiki.stat.ucla.edu/socr/index.php/SOCR_Data_MLB_HeightsWeights`. Retrieved February 20th, 2019.
18. Guyon, Isabelle. 1996. *A Scaling Law for the Validation-Set Training-Set Size Ratio*. AT&T Bell Lab. 1.

3
Supervised Learning

As we learned in the first chapter, supervised learning is one of two major branches of machine learning. In a way, it is similar to how humans learn a new skill: someone else shows us what to do, and we are then able to learn by following their example. In the case of supervised learning algorithms, we usually need lots of examples, that is, lots of data providing the **input** to our algorithm and what the **expected output** should be. The algorithm will learn from this data, and then be able to **predict** the output based on new inputs that it has not seen before.

A surprising number of problems can be addressed using supervised learning. Many email systems use it to classify emails as either important or unimportant automatically whenever a new message arrives in the inbox. More complex examples include image recognition systems, which can identify what an image contains purely from the input pixel values[1]. These systems start by learning from huge datasets of images that have been labelled manually by humans, but are then able to categorize completely new images automatically. It is even possible to use supervised learning to steer a car automatically around a racing track: the algorithm starts by learning how a human driver controls the vehicle, and is eventually able to replicate this behavior[2].

By the end of this chapter, you will be able to use Go to implement two types of supervised learning:

- **Classification**, where an algorithm must learn to classify the input into two or more discrete categories. We will build a simple image recognition system to demonstrate how this works.
- **Regression**, in which the algorithm must learn to predict a continuous variable, for example, the price of an item for sale on a website. For our example, we will predict house prices based on inputs, such as the location, size, and age of the house.

In this chapter, we will be covering the following topics:

- When to use regression and classification
- How to implement regression and classification using Go machine learning libraries
- How to measure the performance of an algorithm

We will cover the two stages involved in building a supervised learning system:

- **Training**, which is the learning phase where we use labelled data to calibrate an algorithm
- **Inference** or **prediction**, where we use the trained algorithm for its intended purpose: to make predictions from input data

Classification

When starting any supervised learning problem, the first step is to load and prepare the data. We are going to start by loading the **MNIST Fashion dataset**[3], a collection of small, grayscale images showing different items of clothing. Our job is to build a system that can recognize what is in each image; that is, does it contain a dress, a shoe, a coat, and so on?

First, we need to download the dataset by running the `download-fashion-mnist.sh` script in the code repository. Then, we will load it into Go:

```
import (
    "fmt"
     mnist "github.com/petar/GoMNIST"
    "github.com/kniren/gota/dataframe"
    "github.com/kniren/gota/series"
    "math/rand"
    "github.com/cdipaolo/goml/linear"
    "github.com/cdipaolo/goml/base"
    "image"
    "bytes"
    "math"
    "github.com/gonum/stat"
    "github.com/gonum/integrate"
)
set, err := mnist.ReadSet("../datasets/mnist/images.gz",
"../datasets/mnist/labels.gz")
```

Let's start by taking a look at a sample of the images. Each one is 28 x 28 pixels, and each pixel has a value between 0 and 255. We are going to use these pixel values as the inputs to our algorithm: our system will accept 784 inputs from an image and use them to classify the image according to which item of clothing it contains. In Jupyter, you can view an image as follows:

```
set.Images[1]
```

This will display one of the 28 x 28 images from the dataset, as shown in the following image:

To make this data suitable for a machine learning algorithm, we need to convert it into a dataframe format, as we learned in Chapter 2, *Setting Up the Development Environment*. To start, we will load the first 1,000 images from the dataset:

```
func MNISTSetToDataframe(st *mnist.Set, maxExamples int)
dataframe.DataFrame {
 length := maxExamples
 if length > len(st.Images) {
 length = len(st.Images)
 }
 s := make([]string, length, length)
 l := make([]int, length, length)
 for i := 0; i < length; i++ {
 s[i] = string(st.Images[i])
 l[i] = int(st.Labels[i])
 }
 var df dataframe.DataFrame
 images := series.Strings(s)
 images.Name = "Image"
 labels := series.Ints(l)
 labels.Name = "Label"
 df = dataframe.New(images, labels)
 return df
}

df := MNISTSetToDataframe(set, 1000)
```

Supervised Learning

We also need a string array that contains the possible labels for each image:

```
categories := []string{"tshirt", "trouser", "pullover", "dress", "coat", "sandal", "shirt", "shoe", "bag", "boot"}
```

It is very important to start by reserving a small proportion of your data in order to test the finished algorithm. This allows us to measure how well the algorithm works on new data that was not used during training. If you do not do this, you will most likely build a system that works really well during training but performs badly when faced with new data. To start with, we are going to use 75% of the images to train our model and 25% of the images to test it.

> **TIP**
> Splitting your data into a **training set** and a **test set** is crucial step when using supervised learning. It is normal to reserve 20-30% of the data for testing, but if your dataset is very large, you may be able to use less than this.

Use the `Split(df dataframe.DataFrame, valFraction float64)` function from the last chapter to prepare these two datasets:

```
training, validation := Split(df, 0.75)
```

A simple model – the logistic classifier

One of the simplest algorithms that solves our problem is a logistic classifier. This is what mathematicians call a **linear model**, which we can understand by thinking about a simple example where we are trying to classify the points on the following two charts as either circles or squares. A linear model will try to do this by drawing a straight line to separate the two types of point. This works very well on the left-hand chart, where the relationship between the inputs (on the chart axes) and the output (circle or square) is simple. However, it does not work on the right-hand chart, where it is not possible to split the points into two correct groups using a straight line:

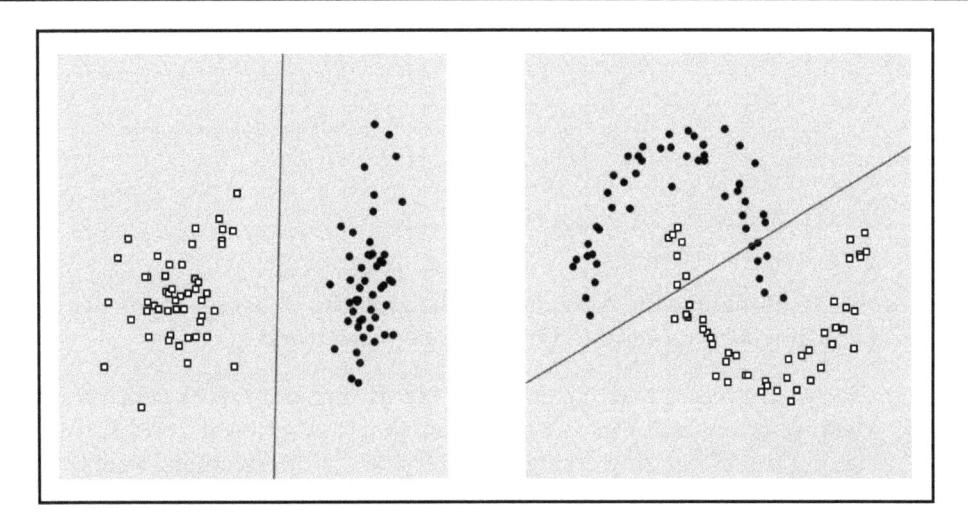

When faced with a new machine learning problem, it is advised that you start with a linear model as a **baseline**, and then compare other models to it. Although linear models ca not capture complex relationships in the input data, they are easy to understand and normally quick to implement and train. You might find that a linear model is good enough for the problem you are working on and save yourself time by not having to implement anything more complex. If not, you can try different algorithms and use the linear model to understand how much better they work.

> A **baseline** is a simple model that you can use as a point of reference when comparing different machine learning algorithms.

Going back to our image dataset, we are going to use a logistic classifier to decide whether an image contains trousers or not. First, let's do some final data preparation: simplify the labels to be either trousers (true) or not-trousers (false):

```
func EqualsInt(s series.Series, to int) (*series.Series, error) {
  eq := make([]int, s.Len(), s.Len())
  ints, err := s.Int()
  if err != nil {
  return nil, err
  }
  for i := range ints {
  if ints[i] == to {
  eq[i] = 1
  }
    }
    ret := series.Ints(eq)
```

Supervised Learning

```
        return &ret, nil
    }

    trainingIsTrouser, err1 := EqualsInt(training.Col("Label"), 1)
    validationIsTrouser, err2 := EqualsInt(validation.Col("Label"), 1)
    if err1 != nil || err2 != nil {
        fmt.Println("Error", err1, err2)
    }
```

We are also going to normalize the pixel data so that, instead of being stored as integers between 0 and 255, it will be represented by floats between 0 and 1:

> **TIP** Many supervised machine learning algorithms only work properly if the data is normalized, that is, rescaled so that it is between 0 and 1. If you are having trouble getting an algorithm to train properly, make sure that you have normalized the data properly.

```
    func NormalizeBytes(bs []byte) []float64 {
        ret := make([]float64, len(bs), len(bs))
        for i := range bs {
            ret[i] = float64(bs[i])/255.
        }
        return ret
    }

    func ImageSeriesToFloats(df dataframe.DataFrame, col string) [][]float64 {
        s := df.Col(col)
        ret := make([][]float64, s.Len(), s.Len())
        for i := 0; i < s.Len(); i++ {
            b := []byte(s.Elem(i).String())
            ret[i] = NormalizeBytes(b)
        }
        return ret
    }

    trainingImages := ImageSeriesToFloats(training, "Image")
    validationImages := ImageSeriesToFloats(validation, "Image")
```

After preparing the data properly, it is finally time to create a logistic classifier and train it:

```
    model := linear.NewLogistic(base.BatchGA, 1e-4, 1, 150, trainingImages,
    trainingIsTrouser.Float())

    //Train
    err := model.Learn()
    if err != nil {
      fmt.Println(err)
    }
```

[58]

Measuring performance

Now that we have our trained model, we need to measure how well it is performing by comparing the predictions it makes on each image with the ground truth (whether or not the image is a pair of trousers). A simple way to do this is to measure **accuracy**.

> **Accuracy** measures what proportion of the input data can be classified correctly by the algorithm, for example, 90%, if 90 out of 100 predictions from the algorithm are correct.

In our Go code example, we can test the model by looping over the validation dataset and counting how many images are classified correctly. This will output a model accuracy of 98.8%:

```
//Count correct classifications
var correct = 0.
for i := range validationImages {
  prediction, err := model.Predict(validationImages[i])
  if err != nil {
    panic(err)
  }

  if math.Round(prediction[0]) == validationIsTrouser.Elem(i).Float() {
    correct++
  }
}

//accuracy
correct / float64(len(validationImages))
```

Precision and recall

Measuring accuracy can be very misleading. Suppose you are building a system to classify whether medical patients will test positive for a rare disease, and in the dataset only 0.1% of examples are in fact positive. A really bad algorithm might predict that nobody will test positive, and yet it has an accuracy of 99.9% simply because the disease is rare.

> A dataset that has many more examples of one classification versus another is known as **unbalanced**. Unbalanced datasets need to be treated carefully when measuring algorithm performance.

Supervised Learning

A better way to measure performance starts by putting each prediction from the algorithm into one of the following four categories:

		Actual output	
		TRUE	FALSE
Model prediction	TRUE	True positive	False positive
	FALSE	False negative	True negative

We can now define some new performance metrics:

- **Precision** measures what fraction of the models true predictions are actually correct. In the following diagram, it is the true positives that are predicted from the model (the left-hand side of the circle) divided by all of the models positive predictions (everything in the circle).
- **Recall** measures how good the model is at identifying all the positive examples. In other words, the true positives (left-hand side of the circle) divided by all the datapoints that are actually positive (the entire left-hand side):

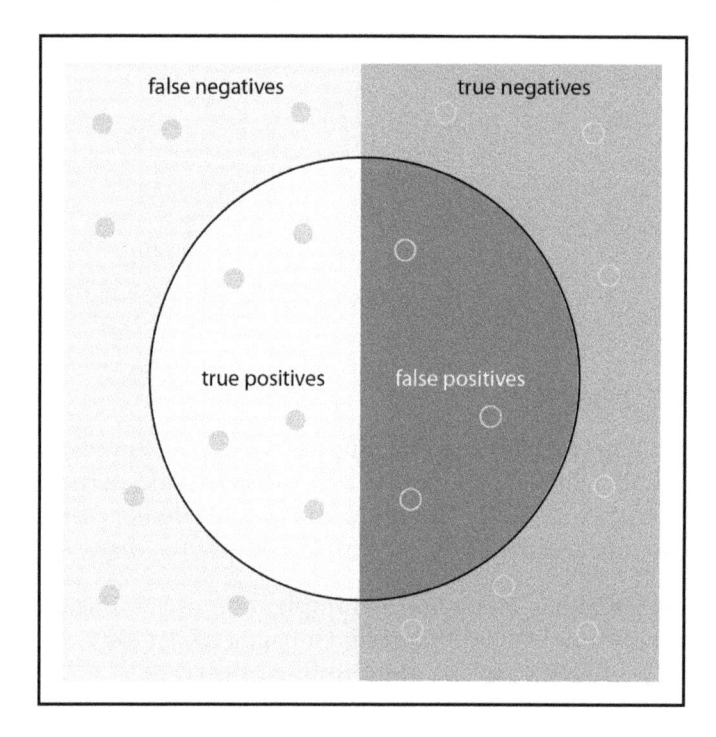

The preceding diagram shows datapoints that have been predicted as true by the model in the central circle. The points that are actually true are on the left half of the diagram.

> **Precision** and **recall** are more robust performance metrics when working with unbalanced datasets. Both range between 0 and 1, where 1 indicates perfect performance.

Following is the code for the total count of true positives and false negatives:

```
//Count true positives and false negatives
var truePositives = 0.
var falsePositives = 0.
var falseNegatives = 0.
for i := range validationImages {
  prediction, err := model.Predict(validationImages[i])
  if err != nil {
    panic(err)
  }
  if validationIsTrouser.Elem(i).Float() == 1 {
    if math.Round(prediction[0]) == 0 {
      // Predicted false, but actually true
      falseNegatives++
    } else {
      // Predicted true, correctly
      truePositives++
    }
  } else {
    if math.Round(prediction[0]) == 1 {
      // Predicted true, but actually false
      falsePositives++
    }
  }
}
```

We can now calculate precision and recall with the following code:

```
//precision
truePositives / (truePositives + falsePositives)
//recall
truePositives / (truePositives + falseNegatives)
```

For our linear model, we get 100% precision, meaning that there are no false positives, and a recall of 90.3%.

Supervised Learning

ROC curves

Another way to measure performance involves looking at how the classifier works in more detail. Inside our model, two things happen:

- First, the model calculates a value between 0 and 1, indicating how likely it is that a given image should be classified as a pair of trousers.
- A threshold is set, so that only images scoring more than the threshold get classified as trousers. Setting different thresholds can improve precision at the expense of recall and vice versa.

If we look at the model output *across all the different thresholds from 0 to 1*, we can understand more about how useful it is. We do this using something called the **receiver operating characteristic** (**ROC**) curve, which is a plot of the true positive rate versus the false positive rate across the dataset for different threshold values. The following three examples show ROC curves for a bad, moderate, and very good classifier:

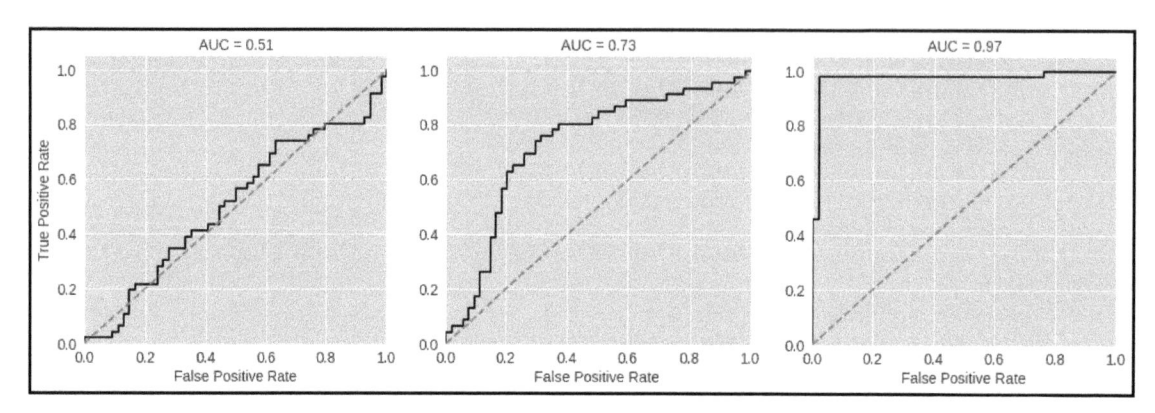

By measuring the shaded area under these ROC curves, we get a simple metric of how good the model is, which is known as **area under curve** (**AUC**). For the bad model, this is close to **0.5**, but for the very good model, it is close to **1.0**, indicating that the model can achieve *both* a high true positive rate and a low false positive rate.

The gonum/stat package provides a useful function for computing ROC curves, which we will use once we have extended the model to work with each of the different items of clothing in the dataset.

> The **receiver operating characteristic**, or **ROC curve**, is a plot of true positive rate versus false positive rate for different threshold values. It allows us to visualize how good the model is at classification. The AUC gives a simple measure of how good the classifier is.

Multi-class models

Up until now, we have been using **binary classification**; that is, it should output `true` if the image shows a pair of trousers, and `false` otherwise. For some problems, such as detecting whether an email is important or not, this is all we need. But in this example, what we really want is a model that can identify all the different types of clothing in our dataset, that is, shirt, boot, dress, and so on.

With some algorithm implementations, you will need to start by applying one-hot encoding to the output, as demonstrated in `Chapter 2`, *Setting Up the Development Environment*. However, for our example, we will use **softmax regression** in **goml/linear**, which does this step automatically. We can train the model by simply feeding it with the input (pixel values) and the integer output (0, 1, 2, ... representing t-shirt, trouser, pullover, and so on):

```
model2 := linear.NewSoftmax(base.BatchGA, 1e-4, 1, 10, 100, trainingImages,
training.Col("Label").Float())

//Train
err := model2.Learn()
if err != nil {
  fmt.Println(err)
}
```

When using this model for inference, it will output a vector of probabilities for each class; that is, it tells us what the probability that an input image is a t-shirt, trouser, and so on. This is exactly what we need for the ROC analysis, but, if we want a single prediction for each image, we can use the following func to find the class that has the *highest* probability:

```
func MaxIndex(f []float64) (i int) {
  var (
    curr float64
    ix int = -1
  )
  for i := range f {
    if f[i] > curr {
      curr = f[i]
      ix = i
    }
  }
  return ix
}
```

Supervised Learning

Next, we can plot the ROC curve and the AUC for each individual class. The following code will loop over each example in the validation dataset and predict probabilities for each class using the new model:

```
//create objects for ROC generation
//as per https://godoc.org/github.com/gonum/stat#ROC
y := make([][]float64, len(categories), len(categories))
classes := make([][]bool, len(categories), len(categories))
//Validate
for i := 0; i < validation.Col("Image").Len(); i++ {
  prediction, err := model2.Predict(validationImages[i])
  if err != nil {
    panic(err)
  }
  for j := range categories {
    y[j] = append(y[j], prediction[j])
    classes[j] = append(classes[j], validation.Col("Label").Elem(i).Float() != float64(j))
  }
}

//Calculate ROC
tprs := make([][]float64, len(categories), len(categories))
fprs := make([][]float64, len(categories), len(categories))

for i := range categories {
  stat.SortWeightedLabeled(y[i], classes[i], nil)
  tprs[i], fprs[i] = stat.ROC(0, y[i], classes[i], nil)
}
```

We can now compute AUC values for each class, which shows that our model performs better on some classes than others:

```
for i := range categories {
  fmt.Println(categories[i])
  auc := integrate.Trapezoidal(fprs[i], tprs[i])
  fmt.Println(auc)
}
```

For trousers, the AUC value is 0.96, showing that even a simple linear model works really well in this case. However, shirt and pullover both score close to 0.6. This makes intuitive sense: shirts and pullovers look very similar, and are therefore much harder for the model to recognize correctly. We can see this more clearly by plotting the ROC curve for each class as separate lines: the model clearly performs the worst on shirts and pullovers, and the best on the clothes that have a very distinctive shape (boots, trousers, sandals, and so on).

The following code loads gonums plotting libraries, creates the ROC plot, and saves it as a JPEG image:

```
import (
  "gonum.org/v1/plot"
  "gonum.org/v1/plot/plotter"
  "gonum.org/v1/plot/plotutil"
  "gonum.org/v1/plot/vg"
  "bufio"
)

func plotROCBytes(fprs, tprs [][]float64, labels []string) []byte {
  p, err := plot.New()
  if err != nil {
    panic(err)
  }

  p.Title.Text = "ROC Curves"
  p.X.Label.Text = "False Positive Rate"
  p.Y.Label.Text = "True Positive Rate"

  for i := range labels {
    pts := make(plotter.XYs, len(fprs[i]))
    for j := range fprs[i] {
      pts[j].X = fprs[i][j]
      pts[j].Y = tprs[i][j]
    }
    lines, points, err := plotter.NewLinePoints(pts)
    if err != nil {
      panic(err)
    }
    lines.Color = plotutil.Color(i)
    lines.Width = 2
    points.Shape = nil

    p.Add(lines, points)
    p.Legend.Add(labels[i], lines, points)
  }

  w, err := p.WriterTo(5*vg.Inch, 4*vg.Inch, "jpg")
  if err != nil {
    panic(err)
  }
  if err := p.Save(5*vg.Inch, 4*vg.Inch, "Multi-class ROC.jpg"); err != nil {
    panic(err)
  }
  var b bytes.Buffer
```

```
    writer := bufio.NewWriter(&b)
    w.WriteTo(writer)
    return b.Bytes()
}
```

If we view the plot in Jupyter, we can see that the the worst classes follow the lines close to the diagonal, again indicating an AUC close to `0.5`:

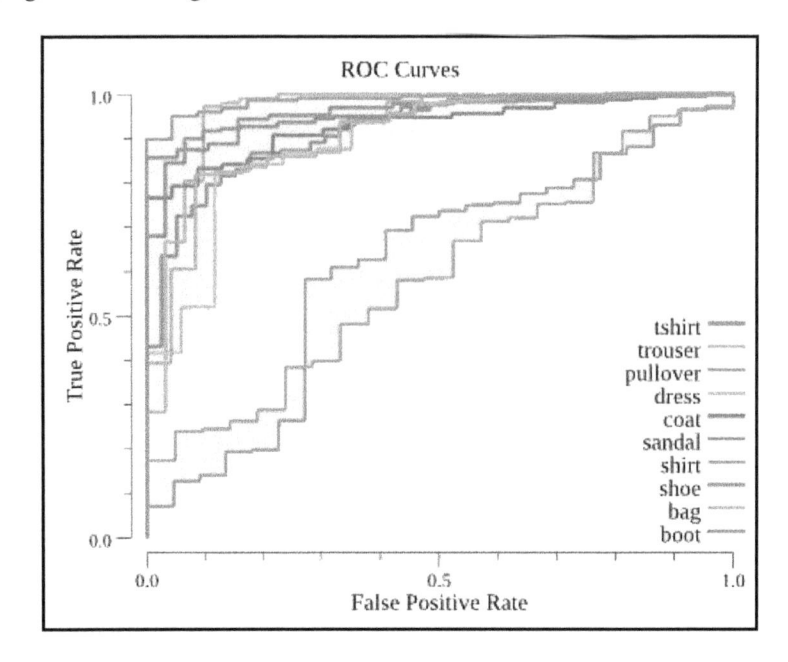

A non-linear model – the support vector machine

To move forward, we need to use a different machine learning algorithm: one that is able to model more complex, non-linear relationships between the pixel inputs and the output classes. While some of the mainstream Go machine learning libraries such as Golearn have support for basic algorithms like local least squares, there is not a single library that supports as broad a set of algorithms as Python's scikit-learn or R's standard library. For this reason, it is often necessary to search for alternative libraries that implement bindings to a widely used C library, or that contain a configurable implementation of an algorithm that is suited for a particular problem. For this example, we are going to use an algorithm called the **support vector machine** (**SVM**). SVMs can be more difficult to use than linear models—they have more parameters to tune—but have the advantage of being able to model much more complex patterns in the data.

> An SVM is a more advanced machine learning method that can be used both for classification and regression. They allow us to apply **kernels** to the input data, which means that they can model non-linear relationships between the inputs/outputs.

An important feature of SVM models is their ability to use a **kernel function**. Put simply, this means that the algorithm can apply a transformation to the input data so that non-linear patterns can be found. For our example, we will use the **LIBSVM** library to train an SVM on the image data. LIBSVM is an open source library with bindings for many different languages, meaning that it is also useful if you want to port a model that has been built in Python's popular scikit-learn library. First, we need to do some data preparation to make our input/output data suitable for feeding into the Go library:

```
trainingOutputs := make([]float64, len(trainingImages))
validationOutputs := make([]float64, len(validationImages))

ltCol:= training.Col("Label")
for i := range trainingImages {
    trainingOutputs[i] = ltCol.Elem(i).Float()
}

lvCol:= validation.Col("Label")
for i := range validationImages {
    validationOutputs[i] = lvCol.Elem(i).Float()
}

// FloatstoSVMNode converts a slice of float64 to SVMNode with sequential
indices starting at 1
func FloatsToSVMNode(f []float64) []libsvm.SVMNode {
    ret := make([]libsvm.SVMNode, len(f), len(f))
    for i := range f {
        ret[i] = libsvm.SVMNode{
            Index: i+1,
            Value: f[i],
        }
    }
    //End of Vector
    ret = append(ret, libsvm.SVMNode{
        Index: -1,
        Value: 0,
    })
    return ret
}
```

Supervised Learning

Next, we can set up the SVM model and configure it with a **radial basis function** (**RBF**) **kernel**. RBF kernels are a common choice when using SVMs, but do take longer to train than linear models:

```
var (
  trainingProblem libsvm.SVMProblem
  validationProblem libsvm.SVMProblem
)

trainingProblem.L = len(trainingImages)
validationProblem.L = len(validationImages)
for i := range trainingImages {
  trainingProblem.X = append(trainingProblem.X,
FloatsToSVMNode(trainingImages[i]))
}
trainingProblem.Y = trainingOutputs

for i := range validationImages {
  validationProblem.X = append(validationProblem.X,
FloatsToSVMNode(validationImages[i]))
}
validationProblem.Y = validationOutputs

// configure SVM
svm := libsvm.NewSvm()
param := libsvm.SVMParameter{
  SvmType: libsvm.CSVC,
  KernelType: libsvm.RBF,
  C: 100,
  Gamma: 0.01,
  Coef0: 0,
  Degree: 3,
  Eps: 0.001,
  Probability: 1,
}
```

Finally, we can fit our model to the training data of 750 images, and then use `svm.SVMPredictProbability` to predict probabilities, like we did with the linear multi-class model:

```
model := svm.SVMTrain(&trainingProblem, &param)
```

As we did previously, we compute the AUC and ROC curves, which demonstrate that this model performs much better across the board, including the difficult classes, like shirt and pullover:

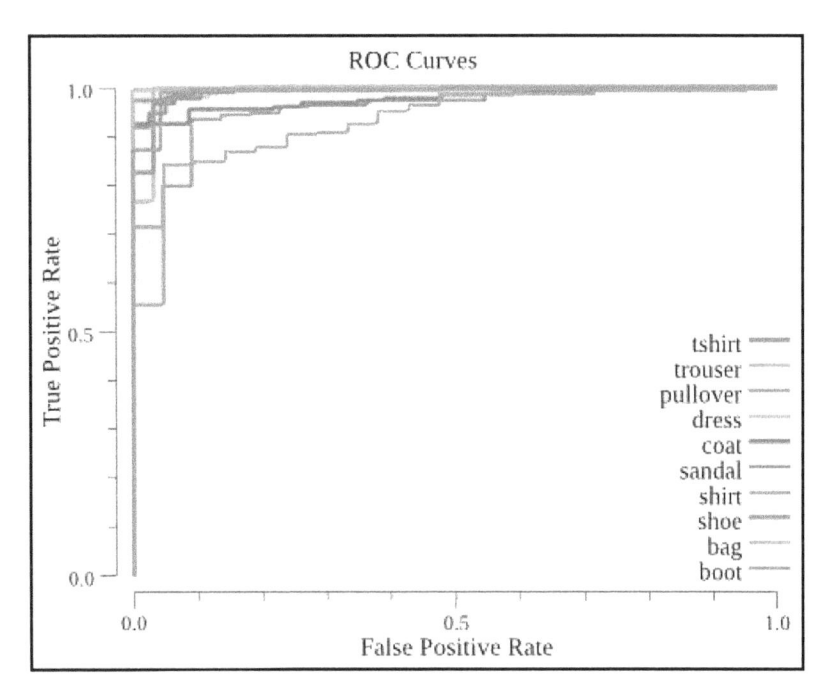

Overfitting and underfitting

The SVM model is performing much better on our validation dataset than the linear model, but, in order to understand what to do next, we need to introduce two important concepts in machine learning: **overfitting** and **underfitting**. These both refer to problems that can occur when training a model.

> If a model **underfits** the data, it is *too simple* to explain the patterns in the input data, and therefore performs poorly when evaluated against the training dataset and the validation dataset. Another term for this problem is that the model has **high bias**.
>
> If a model **overfits** the data, it is *too complex*, and will not generalize well to new data points that were not included as part of training. This means that the model will perform well when evaluated against the training data, but poorly when evaluated against the validation dataset. Another term for this problem is that the model has **high variance**.

Supervised Learning

An easy way to understand the difference between overfitting and underfitting is to look at the following simple example: when building a model, our aim is to build something that is just right for the dataset. The example on the left underfits because a straight line model can not accurately divide the circles and squares. The model on the right is too complex: it separates all the circles and squares correctly, but is unlikely to work well on new data:

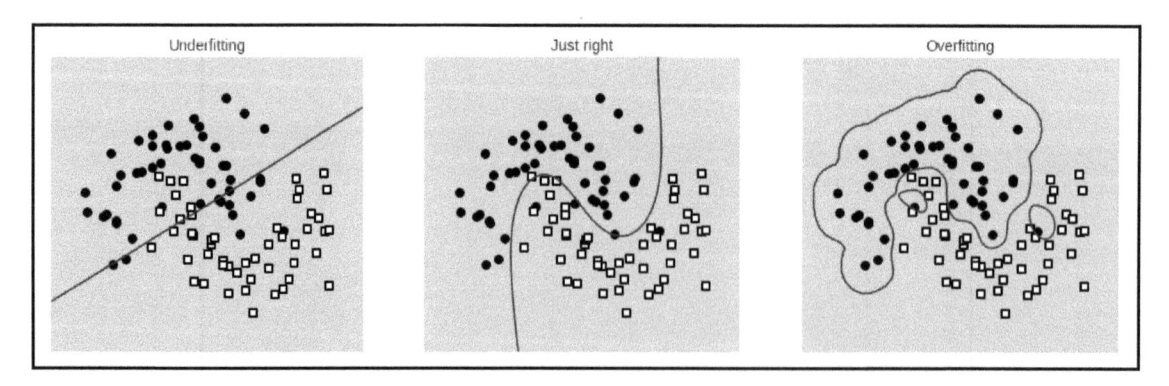

Our linear model suffered from underfitting: it was too simplistic to model the difference between all the classes. Looking at the accuracy of the SVM, we can see that it scores 100% on the training data, but only 82% on validation. This is a clear sign that it is overfitting: it is much worse at classifying new images compared with those on which it was trained.

> **TIP**
> One way of dealing with overfitting is to use more training data: even a complex model will not be able to overfit if the training dataset is large enough. Another way to do this is to introduce regularization: many machine learning models have a parameter that you can adjust to reduce overfitting.

Deep learning

So far, we have improved our model's performance using an SVM, but still face two problems:

- Our SVM is overfitting the training data.
- It is also difficult to scale to the full dataset of 60,000 images: try training the last example with more images and you will find that it gets *much slower*. If we double the number of datapoints, the SVM algorithm takes *more than double* the amount of time.

In this section, we are going to tackle this problem using a **deep neural network**. These types of model have been able to achieve state-of-the-art performance on image classification tasks, as well many other machine learning problems. They are able to model complex non-linear patterns, and also scale well to large datasets.

Data scientists will often use Python to develop and train neural networks because it has access to extremely well-supported deep learning frameworks such as **TensorFlow** and **Keras**. These frameworks make it easier than ever to build complex neural networks and train them on large datasets. They are usually the best choice for building sophisticated deep learning models. In Chapter 5, *Using Pre-Trained Models*, we will look at how to export a trained model from Python and then call it from Go for inference. In this section, we will build a much simpler neural network from scratch using the go-deep library to demonstrate the key concepts.

Neural networks

The basic building block of a neural network is a **neuron** (also known as a **perceptron**). This is actually just the same as our simple linear model: it combines all of its inputs, that is, $x_1, x_2, x_3...$ and so on into a single output, y, according to the following formula:

$$y = w_0 + w_1 * x_1 + w_2 * x_2 + ...$$

The magic of neural networks comes from what happens when we combine these simple neurons:

1. First, we create a **layer** of many neurons into which we feed the input data.
2. At the output of each neuron, we introduce an **activation function**.
3. The output of this **input layer** is then fed to another layer of neurons and activations, known as a **hidden layer**.
4. This gets repeated for multiple hidden layers—the more layers there are, the **deeper** the network is said to be.
5. A final **output** layer of neurons combines the result of the network into the final output.
6. Using a technique known as **backpropagation**, we can train the network by finding the weights, $w_0, w_1, w_2...$, for each neural network that allows the whole network to fit the training data.

Supervised Learning

The following diagram shows this layout: the arrows represent the output of each neuron, which are feeding into the input of the neurons in the next layer:

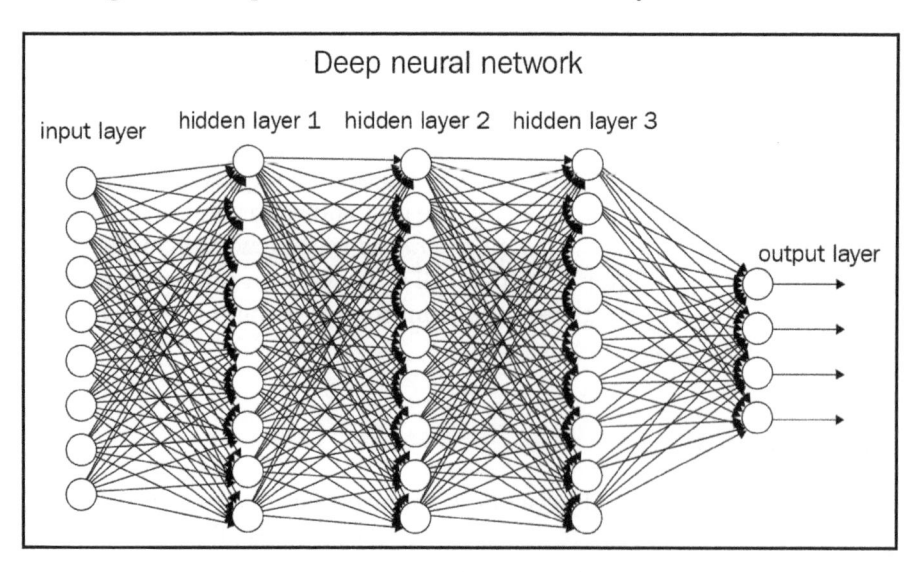

Deep neural network

The neurons in this network are said to be arranged **fully-connected** or **dense** layers. Recent advances in both computing power and software have allowed researchers to build and train more complex neural network architectures than ever before. For instance, a state-of-the-art image recognition system might contain millions of individual weights, and require many days of computing time to train all of these parameters to fit a large dataset. They often contain different arrangements of neurons, for instance, in **convolutional layers**, which perform more specialized learning in these types of systems.

Much of the skill that is required to use deep learning successfully in practice involves a broad understanding of how to select and tune a network to get good performance. There are many blogs and online resources that provide more detail on how these networks work and the types of problems that they have been applied to.

> A **fully-connected** layer in a neural network is one where the inputs of each neuron are connected to the outputs of all the neurons in the previous layer.

A simple deep learning model architecture

Much of the skill in building a successful deep learning model involves choosing the correct model architecture: the number/size/type of layers, and the activation functions for each neuron. Before starting, it is worth researching to see if someone else has already tackled a similar problem to yours using deep learning and published an architecture that works well. As always, it is best to start with something simple and then modify the network iteratively to improve its performance.

For our example, we will start with the following architecture:

- An input layer
- Two hidden layers containing 128 neurons each
- An output layer of 10 neurons (one for each output class in the dataset)
- Each neuron in the hidden layer will use a **rectified linear unit** (**ReLU**) as its output function

> **TIP**
>
> ReLUs are a common choice of activation function in neural networks. They are a very simple way to introduce non-linearity into a model. Other common activation functions include the **logistic** function and the **tanh** function.

The `go-deep` library lets us build this architecture very quickly:

```
import (
 "github.com/patrikeh/go-deep"
 "github.com/patrikeh/go-deep/training"
)

network := deep.NewNeural(&deep.Config{
 // Input size: 784 in our case (number of pixels in each image)
 Inputs: len(trainingImages[0]),
 // Two hidden layers of 128 neurons each, and an output layer 10 neurons (one for each class)
 Layout: []int{128, 128, len(categories)},
 // ReLU activation to introduce some additional non-linearity
 Activation: deep.ActivationReLU,
 // We need a multi-class model
 Mode: deep.ModeMultiClass,
 // Initialise the weights of each neuron using normally distributed random numbers
 Weight: deep.NewNormal(0.5, 0.1),
 Bias: true,
})
```

Neural network training

Training a neural network is another area in which you need to make skillful adjustments in order to get good results. The training algorithm works by calculating how well the model fits a small **batch** of training data (known as the **loss**), and then making small adjustments to the weights to improve the fit. This process then gets repeated over and over again on different batches of training data. The **learning rate** is an important parameter that controls how quickly the algorithm will adjust the neuron weights.

> When training a neural network, the algorithm will feed all of the input data into the network repeatedly, and adjust the network weights as it goes. Each full pass through the data is known as an **epoch**.

> When training a neural network, monitor the **accuracy** and **loss** of the network after each epoch (accuracy should increase, while loss should decrease). If the accuracy is not improving, try lowering the learning rate. Keep training the network until accuracy stops improving: at this point, the network is said to have **converged**.

The following code trains our model using a learning rate of 0.006 for 500 iterations and prints out the accuracy after each epoch:

```
// Parameters: learning rate, momentum, alpha decay, nesterov
optimizer := training.NewSGD(0.006, 0.1, 1e-6, true)
trainer := training.NewTrainer(optimizer, 1)

trainer.Train(network, trainingExamples, validationExamples, 500)
// training, validation, iterations
```

This neural network provides an accuracy of 80% on both the training and validation datasets, a good sign that the model is not overfitting. See if you can improve its performance by adjusting the network architecture and retraining. In Chapter 5, *Using Pre-Trained Models*, we will revisit this example by building a more sophisticated neural network in Python and then exporting it to Go.

Regression

Having mastered many of the key machine learning concepts in the *Classification* section, in this section, we will apply what we have learned to a regression problem. We will be using a dataset containing information about groups of houses in different locations in California[4]. Our goal will be to predict the median house price in each group using input data such as the latitude/longitude location, median house size, age, and so on.

Use the `download-housing.sh` script to download the dataset and then load it into Go:

```
import (
    "fmt"
    "github.com/kniren/gota/dataframe"
    "github.com/kniren/gota/series"
    "math/rand"
    "image"
    "bytes"
    "math"
    "github.com/gonum/stat"
    "github.com/gonum/integrate"
    "github.com/sajari/regression"
    "io/ioutil"
)

const path = "../datasets/housing/CaliforniaHousing/cal_housing.data"

columns := []string{"longitude", "latitude", "housingMedianAge",
"totalRooms", "totalBedrooms", "population", "households", "medianIncome",
"medianHouseValue"}
b, err := ioutil.ReadFile(path)
if err != nil {
    fmt.Println("Error!", err)
}
df := dataframe.ReadCSV(bytes.NewReader(b), dataframe.Names(columns...))
```

We need to carry out some data preparation to create columns in the dataframe that represent the average number of rooms and bedrooms for houses in each area, along with the average occupancy. We will also rescale the median house value into units of $100,000:

```
// Divide divides two series and returns a series with the given name. The
series must have the same length.
func Divide(s1 series.Series, s2 series.Series, name string) series.Series
{
    if s1.Len() != s2.Len() {
        panic("Series must have the same length!")
    }
    ret := make([]interface{}, s1.Len(), s1.Len())
```

Supervised Learning

```
        for i := 0; i < s1.Len(); i ++ {
            ret[i] = s1.Elem(i).Float()/s2.Elem(i).Float()
        }
        s := series.Floats(ret)
        s.Name = name
        return s
}

// MultiplyConst multiplies the series by a constant and returns another
series with the same name.
func MultiplyConst(s series.Series, f float64) series.Series {
        ret := make([]interface{}, s.Len(), s.Len())
        for i := 0; i < s.Len(); i ++ {
            ret[i] = s.Elem(i).Float()*f
        }
        ss := series.Floats(ret)
        ss.Name = s.Name
        return ss
}

df = df.Mutate(Divide(df.Col("totalRooms"), df.Col("households"),
"averageRooms"))
df = df.Mutate(Divide(df.Col("totalBedrooms"), df.Col("households"),
"averageBedrooms"))
df = df.Mutate(Divide(df.Col("population"), df.Col("households"),
"averageOccupancy"))
df = df.Mutate(MultiplyConst(df.Col("medianHouseValue"), 0.00001))
df = df.Select([]string{"medianIncome", "housingMedianAge", "averageRooms",
"averageBedrooms", "population", "averageOccupancy", "latitude",
"longitude", "medianHouseValue" })
```

Like we did previously, we need to split this data into training and validation sets:

```
func Split(df dataframe.DataFrame, valFraction float64) (training
dataframe.DataFrame, validation dataframe.DataFrame){
        perm := rand.Perm(df.Nrow())
        cutoff := int(valFraction*float64(len(perm)))
        training = df.Subset(perm[:cutoff])
        validation = df.Subset(perm[cutoff:])
        return training, validation
}

training, validation := Split(df, 0.75)

// DataFrameToXYs converts a dataframe with float64 columns to a slice of
independent variable columns as floats
// and the dependent variable (yCol). This can then be used with eg. goml's
linear ML algorithms.
```

```
// yCol is optional - if it does not exist only the x (independent)
variables will be returned.
func DataFrameToXYs(df dataframe.DataFrame, yCol string) ([][]float64,
[]float64){
    var (
        x [][]float64
        y []float64
        yColIx = -1
    )
    //find dependent variable column index
    for i, col := range df.Names() {
        if col == yCol {
            yColIx = i
            break
        }
    }
    if yColIx == -1 {
        fmt.Println("Warning - no dependent variable")
    }
    x = make([][]float64, df.Nrow(), df.Nrow())
    y = make([]float64, df.Nrow())
    for i := 0; i < df.Nrow(); i++ {
        var xx []float64
        for j := 0; j < df.Ncol(); j ++ {
            if j == yColIx {
                y[i] = df.Elem(i, j).Float()
                continue
            }
            xx = append(xx, df.Elem(i,j).Float())
        }
        x[i] = xx
    }
    return x, y
}

trainingX, trainingY := DataFrameToXYs(training, "medianHouseValue")
validationX, validationY := DataFrameToXYs(validation, "medianHouseValue")
```

Linear regression

Like the classification example, we are going to start by using a linear model as a baseline. This time, though, we are predicting a **continuous output variable**, so we need a different performance metric. A common metric to use for regression is the **mean squared error** (**MSE**), that is, the sum of the squared differences between the model predictions and the true values. By using a *squared* error, we are making sure that the value increases for underestimates and overestimates are of the true value.

> **TIP**: A common alternative to MSE for regression problems is the **mean absolute error** (**MAE**). This can be useful when your input data contains outliers.

Using a Golang regression library, we can train the model as follows:

```
model := new(regression.Regression)

for i := range trainingX {
  model.Train(regression.DataPoint(trainingY[i], trainingX[i]))
}
if err := model.Run(); err != nil {
  fmt.Println(err)
}
```

Finally, we can calculate the mean squared error from the validation set as 0.51. This provides a benchmark level of performance that we can refer to when comparing other models:

```
//On validation set
errors := make([]float64, len(validationX), len(validationX))
for i := range validationX {
  prediction, err := model.Predict(validationX[i])
  if err != nil {
    panic(fmt.Println("Prediction error", err))
  }
  errors[i] = (prediction - validationY[i]) * (prediction - validationY[i])
}

fmt.Printf("MSE: %5.2f\n", stat.Mean(errors, nil))
```

Random forest regression

We know that house prices vary according to location, often in complicated ways that our linear model is unlikely to be able to capture. Therefore, we are going to introduce **random forest regression** as an alternative model.

> **Random forest regression** is an example of an **ensemble model**: it works by training a large number of simple **base models** and then uses statistical averaging to output a final prediction. With random forests, the base models are decision trees, and, by adjusting the parameters of these trees and the number of models in the ensemble, you can control overfitting.

Using the RF.go library, we can train a random forest on the house price data. First, let's do some data preparation on the training and validation sets:

```
func FloatsToInterfaces(f []float64) []interface{} {
    iif := make([]interface{}, len(f), len(f))
    for i := range f {
        iif[i] = f[i]
    }
    return iif
}

tx, trainingY := DataFrameToXYs(training, "medianHouseValue")
vx, validationY := DataFrameToXYs(validation, "medianHouseValue")

var (
    trainingX = make([][]interface{}, len(tx), len(tx))
    validationX = make([][]interface{}, len(vx), len(vx))
)

for i := range tx {
    trainingX[i] = FloatsToInterfaces(tx[i])
}
for i := range vx {
    validationX[i] = FloatsToInterfaces(vx[i])
}
```

Now, we can fit a random forest containing 25 underlying decision trees:

```
model := Regression.BuildForest(trainingX, trainingY, 25, len(trainingX), 1)
```

This gives a much improved MSE of 0.29 on the validation set, but shows signs of overfitting with an error of only 0.05 on the training data.

Other regression models

There are many other regression models you can try out on this dataset. In fact, the SVM and deep learning models that we used in the previous example can also be adapted for use on regression problems. See if you can improve on the performance of the random forest by using a different model. Remember that some of these models will require the data to be normalized so that they can be trained properly.

Summary

We have covered a lot of ground in this chapter, and introduced many important machine learning concepts. The first step in tackling a supervised learning problem is to collect and preprocess the data, making sure that it is normalized, and split into training and validation sets. We covered a range of different algorithms for both classification and regression. In each example, there were two phases: training the algorithm, followed by inference; that is, using the trained model to make predictions from new input data. Whenever you try a new machine learning technique on your data, it is important to keep track of its performance against the training and validation datasets. This serves two main purposes: it helps you diagnose underfitting/overfitting and also provides an indication of how well your model is working.

It is usually best to choose the simplest model that provides good enough performance for the task that you are working on. Simple models are usually faster and easier to implement and use. In each example, we started with a simple linear model, and then evaluated more sophisticated techniques against this baseline.

There are many different implementations of machine learning models for Go that are available online. As we have done in this chapter, it is usually quicker to find and use an existing library rather than implementing an algorithm completely from scratch. Often, these libraries have slightly different requirements in terms of data preparation and tuning parameters, so be sure to read the documentation carefully in each case.

The next chapter will reuse many of the techniques for data loading and preparation that we have implemented here, but, instead, will focus on unsupervised machine learning.

Further readings

1. `http://yann.lecun.com/exdb/lenet/`. Retrieved March 24, 2019.
2. `https://blogs.nvidia.com/blog/2016/05/06/self-driving-cars-3/`. Retrieved March 24, 2019.
3. `https://github.com/zalandoresearch/fashion-mnist`. Retrieved March 24, 2019.
4. `http://colah.github.io/`. Retrieved May 15, 2019.
5. `https://karpathy.github.io/`. Retrieved May 15, 2019.
6. `http://www.dcc.fc.up.pt/~ltorgo/Regression/cal_housing.html`. Retrieved March 24, 2019.

4
Unsupervised Learning

While the majority of machine learning problems involve labeled data, as we saw in the previous chapter, there is another important branch called **unsupervised learning**. This applies in situations where you may not have labels for the input data, and so the algorithm cannot work by trying to predict output labels from each input. Instead, unsupervised algorithms work by trying to spot patterns or structure in the input. It can be a useful technique when carrying out exploratory analysis on a large dataset with many different input variables. In this situation, it would be incredibly time-consuming to plot charts of all the different variables to try to spot patterns, so instead, unsupervised learning can be used to do this automatically.

As humans, we are very familiar with this concept: much of what we do is never explicitly taught to us by someone else. Instead, we explore the world around us, looking for, and discovering, patterns. For this reason, unsupervised learning is of particular interest to researchers who are trying to develop systems for **general intelligence**: computers that can learn what they need independently[1].

In this chapter, we are going to introduce two popular unsupervised algorithms and implement them in Go. First, we will use a **clustering algorithm** to separate a dataset into distinct groups without any guidance about what to look for. Then, we will use a technique called **principal component analysis** to compress a dataset by first finding hidden structures within it.

This will just scratch the surface of what unsupervised learning is able to achieve. Some cutting-edge algorithms are able to allow computers to carry out tasks that normally require human creativity. One example worth looking at is NVIDIA's system for creating realistic pictures from sketches[2]. You can also find code examples online for networks that can make realistic changes to how an image appears, for instance, turning horses into zebras, or oranges into apples[3].

The following topics will be covered in this chapter:

- Clustering
- Principal component analysis

Clustering

Clustering algorithms are designed to split a dataset up into groups. Once trained, any new data can be assigned to a group when it arrives. Suppose you are working with a dataset of customer information for an e-commerce store. You might use clustering to identify groups of customers, for example, business/private customers. This information can then be used to make decisions about how to best serve those customer types.

You might also use clustering as a preparatory step before applying supervised learning. For example, a dataset of images may require manual labeling, which is often time-consuming and costly. If you can segment the dataset into groups with a clustering algorithm, then you may be able to save time by only labeling a fraction of the images, and then assuming that each cluster contains images with the same label.

Clustering has also been applied to computer vision applications in autonomous vehicles, where it can be used to help a vehicle navigate on an unknown stretch of road. By clustering the data from the vehicles cameras, it is possible to identify which area of each incoming image contains the road on which the vehicle must drive[4].

For our example, we are going to use a dataset containing measurements of different types of iris flower, which you can download using the `./download-iris.sh` script in the code repository. This data is often used to demonstrate supervised learning: you can use machine learning to classify the data according to the species of iris flower. In this case, however, we will not provide labels to the clustering algorithm, meaning that it has to identify clusters purely from the measurement data:

1. First, load the data into Go, as we have done in previous examples:

    ```
    import (
      "fmt"
      "github.com/kniren/gota/dataframe"
      "github.com/kniren/gota/series"
      "io/ioutil"
      "bytes"
      "math/rand"
    )

    const path = "../datasets/iris/iris.csv"
    ```

```
        b, err := ioutil.ReadFile(path)
        if err != nil {
            fmt.Println("Error!", err)
        }
        df := dataframe.ReadCSV(bytes.NewReader(b))
        df.SetNames("petal length", "petal width", "sepal length", "sepal
        width", "species")
```

2. Next, we need to prepare the data by splitting the species column from the rest of the data: this will only be used for the final assessment of the groups after clustering. To do this, use the `DataFrameToXYs` func from previous examples:

   ```
   features, classification := DataFrameToXYs(df, "species")
   ```

3. Now, we can train an algorithm called **k-means** to try to split the dataset into three clusters. k-means works by initially choosing the middle (known as the **centroid**) of each cluster at random, and assigning each data point in the training set to its nearest centroid. It then iteratively updates the positions of each cluster, reassigning the data points at each step until it reaches convergence.

> **TIP**: **k-means** is a simple algorithm and is fast to train, so it is a good starting point when clustering data. However, it does require you to specify how many clusters to find, which is not always obvious. Other clustering algorithms, such as DBSCAN, do not have this limitation.

Using the k-means implementation in goml, we can try to find three clusters within the data. Often, you may need to use trial and error to find out how many clusters to use—K. If you have lots of very small clusters after running k-means, then you probably need to reduce K:

```
import (
    "gonum.org/v1/plot"
    "gonum.org/v1/plot/plotter"
    "gonum.org/v1/plot/plotutil"
    "gonum.org/v1/plot/vg"
    "github.com/cdipaolo/goml/cluster"
    "github.com/cdipaolo/goml/base"
    "bufio"
    "strconv"
)

model := cluster.NewKMeans(3, 30, features)

if err := model.Learn(); err != nil {
```

```
        panic(err)
    }
```

Once we have fitted the model to the data, we can generate a prediction from it; that is, find out which cluster each data point belongs to:

```
func PredictionsToScatterData(features [][]float64, model base.Model,
featureForXAxis, featureForYAxis int) (map[int]plotter.XYs) {
    ret := make(map[int]plotter.XYs)
    if features == nil {
        panic("No features to plot")
    }
    for i := range features {
        var pt struct{X, Y float64}
        pt.X = features[i][featureForXAxis]
        pt.Y = features[i][featureForYAxis]
        p, _ := model.Predict(features[i])
        ret[int(p[0])] = append(ret[int(p[0])], pt)
    }
    return ret
}

scatterData := PredictionsToScatterData(features, model, 2, 3)
```

Now, we are able to plot the clusters using the following code:

```
func PredictionsToScatterData(features [][]float64, model base.Model,
featureForXAxis, featureForYAxis int) (map[int]plotter.XYs) {
    ret := make(map[int]plotter.XYs)
    if features == nil {
        panic("No features to plot")
    }
    for i := range features {
        var pt struct{X, Y float64}
        pt.X = features[i][featureForXAxis]
        pt.Y = features[i][featureForYAxis]
        p, _ := model.Predict(features[i])
        ret[int(p[0])] = append(ret[int(p[0])], pt)
    }
    return ret
}

scatterData := PredictionsToScatterData(features, model, 2, 3)
```

Chapter 4

What this does is display the data using two of the input features, Sepal width and Sepal length, as shown in the following diagram:

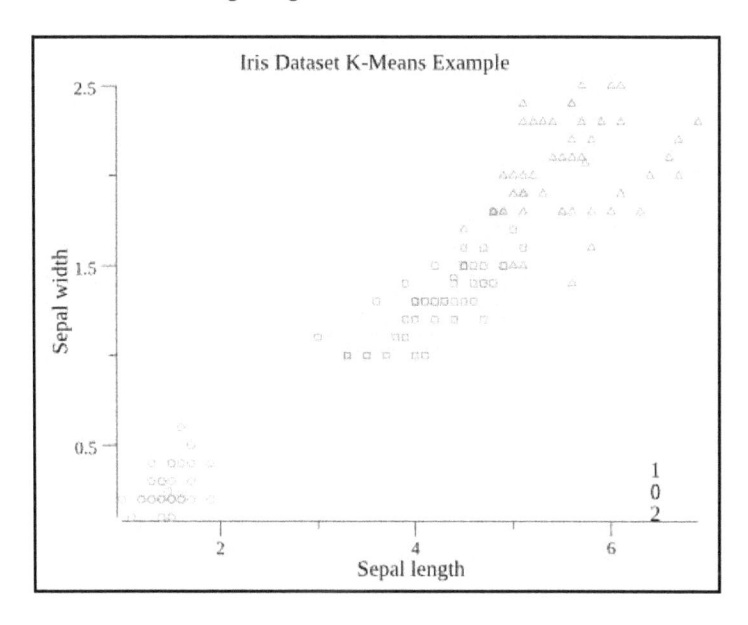

The shape of each point is set according to the iris species, while the color is set by the output of k-means, that is, which cluster the algorithm has assigned each data point to. What we can now see is that the clusters match the species of each iris almost exactly: k-means has been able to subdivide the data into three distinct groups that correspond to the different species.

While k-means works very well in this case, you might find that you need to use a different algorithm on your own datasets. The scikit-learn library for Python comes with a useful demonstration of which algorithms work best on different types of dataset[5]. You might also find that it is helpful to prepare your data in some way; for example, normalize it or apply a non-linear transformation to it.

Unsupervised Learning

Principal component analysis

Principal component analysis (**PCA**) is a way to reduce the number of dimensions in a dataset. We can think of it as a way of compressing a dataset. Suppose you have 100 different variables in your dataset. It may be the case that many of these variables are correlated with each other. If this is the case, then it is possible to explain most of the variation in the data by combining variables to build a smaller set of data. PCA performs this task: it tries to find linear combinations of your input variables, and reports how much variation is explained by each combination.

> PCA is a method for reducing the dimensions in a dataset: in effect, summarizing it so that you can focus on the most important features, which explain most of the variation in the dataset.

PCA can be useful for machine learning in two ways:

- It can be a useful preprocessing step before applying a supervised learning method. After running PCA on your data, you may discover, for instance, that 95% of the variation is explained by only a handful of variables. You can use this knowledge to reduce the number of variables in your input data, which means that your subsequent model will train much faster.
- It can also be helpful when visualizing a dataset prior to building a model. If your data has more than three variables, it can be very hard to visualize it on a graph and understand what patterns it contains. PCA lets you transform the data so that you can plot just the most important aspects of it.

For our example, we are going to use PCA to visualize the iris dataset. Currently, this has four input features: petal width, petal length, sepal width, and sepal length. Using PCA, we can reduce this down to two variables, which we can then visualize easily on a scatter plot.

1. Start by loading the sepal data as before, and normalizing it as follows:

    ```
    df = Standardise(df, "petal length")
    df = Standardise(df, "petal width")
    df = Standardise(df, "sepal length")
    df = Standardise(df, "sepal width")
    labels := df.Col("species").Float()
    df = DropColumn(df, "species")
    ```

2. Next, we need to convert the data into a matrix format. The gonum library has a mat64 type that we can use for this purpose:

   ```
   import (
       "github.com/gonum/matrix/mat64"
   )

   // DataFrameToMatrix converts the given dataframe to a gonum matrix
   func DataFrameToMatrix(df dataframe.DataFrame) mat64.Matrix {
       var x []float64 //slice to hold matrix entries in row-major order
       for i := 0; i < df.Nrow(); i++ {
           for j := 0; j < df.Ncol(); j ++ {
               x = append(x, df.Elem(i,j).Float())
           }
       }
       return mat64.NewDense(df.Nrow(), df.Ncol(), x)
   }

   features := DataFrameToMatrix(df)
   ```

   > PCA works by finding the **eigenvectors** and **eigenvalues** of the dataset. For this reason, most software libraries need the data to be in a matrix structure, so that standard linear algebra routines such as **blas** and **lapack** can be used to do the calculations.

3. Now, we can make use of gonum's stat package for the PCA implementation:

   ```
   model := stat.PC{}
   if ok := model.PrincipalComponents(features, nil); !ok {
     fmt.Println("Error!")
   }
   variances := model.Vars(nil)
   components := model.Vectors(nil)
   ```

   This gives us two variables: components, which is a matrix telling us how to map the original variables to the new components; and variances, which tells us how much variance is explained by each component. If we print out the variance in each component, we can see that the first two explain 96% of the entire dataset (component 1 to 73%, and component 2 to 23%):

   ```
   total_variance := 0.0
   for i := range variances {
     total_variance += variances[i]
   }

   for i := range variances {
   ```

```
        fmt.Printf("Component %d: %5.3f\n", i+1,
        variances[i]/total_variance)
    }
```

4. Finally, we can transform the data into the new components, and keep the first two so that we can use them for visualization:

```
transform := mat64.NewDense(df.Nrow(), 4, nil)
transform.Mul(features, components)

func PCAToScatterData(m mat64.Matrix, labels []float64)
map[int]plotter.XYs {
    ret := make(map[int]plotter.XYs)
    nrows, _ := m.Dims()
    for i := 0; i < nrows; i++ {
        var pt struct{X, Y float64}
        pt.X = m.At(i, 0)
        pt.Y = m.At(i, 1)
        ret[int(labels[i])] = append(ret[int(labels[i])], pt)
    }
    return ret
}

scatterData := PCAToScatterData(transform, labels)
```

The following diagram shows each data point according to the first two principle components, while the colors indicate which iris species each one belongs to. We can now see that the three groups form distinct bands along the first component, which we could not have easily seen when plotting the four original input features against one another:

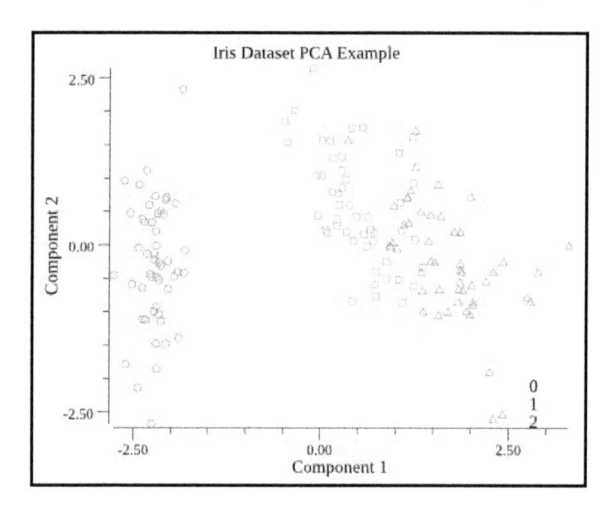

You could now try training a supervised learning model to use the first two PCA features to predict the iris species: compare its performance against a model trained on all four input features.

Summary

In this chapter, we have covered two common techniques in unsupervised machine learning. Both are often used by data scientists for exploratory analysis, but can also form part of a data processing pipeline in a production system. You have learned how to train a clustering algorithm to divide data automatically into groups. This technique might be used to categorize newly registered customers on an e-commerce website, so that they can be served with personalized information. We also introduced principal component analysis as a means of compressing data, in other words, reducing its dimensionality. This may be used as a preprocessing step before running a supervised learning technique in order to reduce the size of the dataset.

In both cases, it is possible to make use of the `gonum` and `goml` libraries to build efficient implementations in Go with minimal code.

Further readings

1. `https://deepmind.com/blog/unsupervised-learning/`. Retrieved April 12, 2019.
2. `https://blogs.nvidia.com/blog/2019/03/18/gaugan-photorealistic-landscapes-nvidia-research/`. Retrieved April 12, 2019.
3. `https://github.com/junyanz/CycleGAN`. Retrieved April 12, 2019.
4. `http://robots.stanford.edu/papers/dahlkamp.adaptvision06.pdf`. Retrieved April 13, 2019.
5. `https://scikit-learn.org/stable/modules/clustering.html#overview-of-clustering-methods`. Retrieved April 12, 2019.

5
Using Pretrained Models

In the previous two chapters, you learned how to use supervised ML algorithms (Chapter 3, *Supervised Learning*) and unsupervised ML algorithms (Chapter 4, *Unsupervised Learning*) to solve a wide range of problems. The solutions created models from scratch and consisted only of Go code. We did not use models that had already been trained, nor did we attempt to call Matlab, Python, or R code from Go. However, there are several situations in which this can be beneficial. In this chapter, we will present several strategies aimed at using pretrained models and creating polyglot ML applications – that is, where the main application logic is written in Go but where specialist techniques and models may have been written in other languages.

In this chapter, you will learn about the following topics:

- How to load a pretrained GoML model and use it to generate a prediction
- When to consider using a pure-Go solution or polyglot solution
- How to use the os/exec package to invoke ML models written in other languages
- How to use HTTP to invoke ML models written in other languages, where they may reside on a different machine or even across the internet
- How to run TensorFlow models using the TensorFlow API for Go

How to restore a saved GoML model

Once you have put the hard work into creating a ML model, you may need to shut down your computer. What happens to your model when the computer is restarted? Unless you have persisted it to disk, it will disappear and you will need to start the training process again. Even if you have saved the model hyperparameters in a gophernotes notebook, the model itself will not have been saved. And if the training process is a long one, you may need to wait a long time before your model is ready to use again.

In the following example, we will explain how to restore the model we created in Chapter 3, *Supervised Learning*, and persist it to the local filesystem in a `model.dat` file using its `PersistToFile` method, which is provided by the GoML API. We will restore it using its `RestoreFromFile` method. We will assume that all the other funcs we created in Chapter 3, *Supervised Learning*, are available to us, such as converting an image into a slice of floats:

```
// IsImageTrousers invokes the Saved model to predict if image at given 
index is, in fact, of trousers
// For simplicity, this loads the model from disk on every request, whereas 
loading it once and caching it
// would be preferable in a commercial application.

func IsImageTrousers(i int) (bool, error) {
  model := linear.Logistic{}
  if err := model.RestoreFromFile("model.dat"); err != nil {
    return false, err
  }
  prediction, err := model.Predict(testImages[i])
  return prediction > 0.5, err
}
```

We can now use this code within gophernotes to generate a prediction and compare it to the ground truth in the `Label` column:

```
// Prediction

IsImageTrousers(16)
```

Running the preceding code cell in gophernotes will produce the following output:

```
true <nil>
```

Let's check the output:

```
// Ground truth
df.Col("Label").Elem(16).Int() == 1
```

We could also use the same validation techniques we introduced in Chapter 3, *Supervised Learning*, to check that the quality of the output is as expected. This approach works very well when the model was written in Go and persisted to be reused at a later time. However, if the model was written in Python and not recoverable directly in Go (such is the case for scikit-learn models, for example), the only way to use it to make a prediction may be to engineer some communication between a Python model and a Go application. While this increases the overall complexity of the applications, it has significant advantages, as we will discuss in the following sections.

Deciding when to adopt a polyglot approach

As we have seen in the previous chapters, the Go ecosystem provides ample opportunities to solve machine learning problems natively. However, being obstinate in requiring the solution to remain pure-Go can lead to increased development time or even reduced training performance, as other, more specialized ML libraries can provide higher-level APIs or performance optimizations that have not been implemented in the corresponding Go libraries yet.

A good example of both is the Python ML library, Keras. The aim of this library is to provide a high-level API that allows the author to perform a wide range of ML tasks, such as data preprocessing, model training, model validation, and persistence. Its abstractions have concrete implementations in various backends, such as TensorFlow, which are known to be extremely performant. For these reasons, Keras is one of the most popular ML libraries in any language: its MIT-licensed GitHub repository has over 40,000 stars and a search on GitHub reveals that over 20,000 repositories match the search term keras, meaning that the name of the repository includes that word. A search of the code content reveals that over one million files on GitHub contain the search term keras.

However, to write the entire application in Python just to make use of one library fails to take advantage of the benefits offered by Go, which we enumerated in Chapter 1, *Introducing Machine Learning with Go*. If these factors are not important in the development of your application, then by all means create it in Python, but, in what follows, we will assume that you want the best of both worlds.

Therefore, two options present themselves: first, develop the application entirely in Go. Second, develop the ML model in Python and invoke this model from your Go code, which will contain the main application and business logic. Within a commercial setting where the goal is to produce a production-ready product, the advantages of both options are as follows:

Pure-Go application:

- Easier to maintain over a polyglot solution
- Less complexity in application component interactions, because there is no need to manage invocation of an external ML component
- Easier to on-board team members
- Less dependencies to update

Existing libraries may offer the required functionality out of the box with sufficient performance, obviating any advantage gained from using specialized libraries in other languages.

Polyglot application:

- Drastically reduce the amount of code for complex ML problems using high-level abstractions from specialist libraries in other languages
- In some cases, performance advantages, as some GoML libraries are not designed for out-and-out speed (deep learning is a good example of this)
- Can suit a multi-team approach better, as data science teams are more familiar with Python or R libraries
- Leverage preexisting models—academic research papers typically publish Caffe or TensorFlow models with Python or Lua scripts to invoke them

In conclusion, for ML applications where existing Go libraries offer what you need out of the box or with little modification, a native Go solution will reduce complexity in the application and enhance maintainability. However, if this is not the case, particularly for very complex problems such as deep learning and computer vision, combining Go with the latest tools from other languages is worth the added complexity.

In the examples that follow, we will invoke a variety of Python ML models from a Go application. Our reason for using Python specifically is that Python is preinstalled in most Linux distributions and is also the most popular language for ML[4][5]. The solutions we will describe can be applied to a model written in any programming language.

Example – invoking a Python model using os/exec

To get started with polyglot ML applications, we will revisit the logistic regression example from `Chapter 3`, *Supervised Learning*. We will assume that, instead of Go, the model was written in Python and that we wish to invoke it from our Go application. To do this, we will use command-line arguments to pass inputs to the model and read the model's prediction from **standard output** (**STDOUT**).

To exchange data between Python and Go, we will use strings formatted using **JavaScript Object Notation** (**JSON**). This choice is arbitrary of course[6], and we could have chosen any one of the other formats for which the Go and Python standard libraries have support, such as XML, or invented our own. JSON has the advantage that it takes very little effort to use in both languages.

The process we will follow to communicate with the Python subprocess is as follows. Generally, there are three steps: serialization of the request, executing the subprocess, and deserialization of the response:

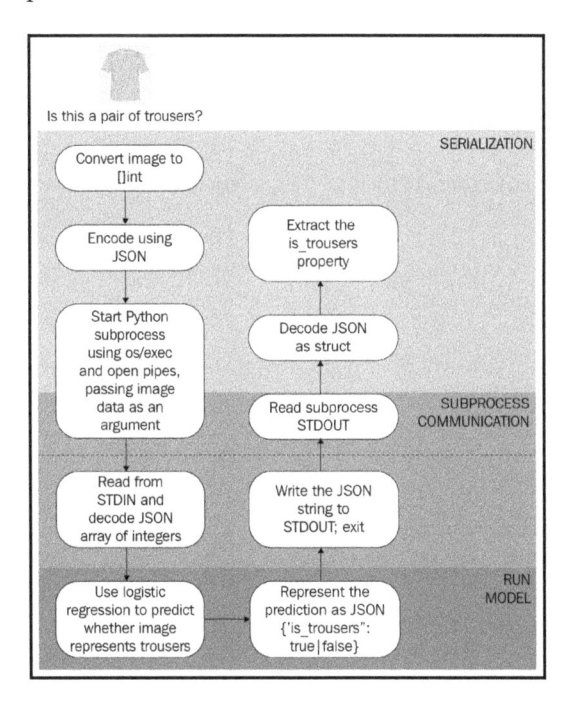

Fig.1: The process we use to communicate with a Python subprocess that runs a pretrained logistic regression model

Using Pretrained Models

We will start by loading the MNIST dataset and converting it into a dataframe. You can find the code for this in `Chapter 3`, *Supervised Learning*. This time, however, we will convert the image data into a slice of ints, with each int between 0 and 255 (the value of each pixel), rather than a slice of floats. This is to ensure alignment with the Python model:

```
// ImageSeriesToInts converts the dataframe's column containing image data
for multiple images to a slice of int slices, where each int is between 0
and 255, representing the value of the pixel.

func ImageSeriesToInts(df dataframe.DataFrame, col string) [][]int {

  s := df.Col(col)

  ret := make([][]int, s.Len(), s.Len())

  for i := 0; i < s.Len(); i++ {

    b := []byte(s.Elem(i).String())

    ret[i] = NormalizeBytes(b)

  }

  return ret

}
```

Next, we will introduce a function that will allow us to start the Python subprocess and wait for it to finish:

```
// InvokeAndWait invokes a Python 3 script with the given arguments, waits
for it to finish, and returns the concatenated output of its STDOUT and
STERRR.
func InvokeAndWait(args ...string) ([]byte, error) {
  var (
    output []byte
    errOutput []byte
    err error
  )
  cmd := exec.Command("python3", args...)
  stdout, err := cmd.StdoutPipe()
  if err != nil {
    return nil, err
  }
  stderr, err := cmd.StderrPipe()
  if err := cmd.Start(); err != nil {
    return nil, err
  }
```

```
    if output, err = ioutil.ReadAll(stdout); err != nil {
      return nil, err
    }
    if errOutput, err = ioutil.ReadAll(stderr); err != nil || len(errOutput) > 0 {
      return nil, fmt.Errorf("Error running model: %s", string(errOutput))
    }
    return output, nil
}
```

Now, we are ready to assemble our prediction function, which will serialize the image data, pass it to the subprocess as an argument when it starts, wait for the subprocess to finish, and deserialize the response:

```
// IsImageTrousers invokes the Python model to predict if image at given index is, in fact, of trousers

func IsImageTrousers(i int) (bool, error){
    b, err := json.Marshal(testImages[i])
    if err != nil {
        panic(err)
    }
    b, err = InvokeAndWait("model.py", "predict", string(b))
    if err != nil {
        return false, err
    } else {
        var ret struct {
            IsTrousers bool `json:"is_trousers"`
        }
        err := json.Unmarshal(b, &ret)
        if err != nil {
            return false, err
        }
        return ret.IsTrousers, nil
    }
}
```

We can now use this code within gophernotes to generate a prediction and compare it to the ground truth in the `Label` column:

```
// Prediction
IsImageTrousers(16)
```

Running this in a gophernotes cell provides the following output:

```
true <nil>
```

Let's check the output:

```
// Ground truth
df.Col("Label").Elem(16).Int() == 1
```

As expected, this outputs `true`. We can repeat this for several different images to get some confidence that everything is working as it should. Both the Go and Python code use the `predict` argument to signify which action should be performed – we could also have a `test` action that checks that the image the Python code reconstructs from its arguments is the correct one, further increasing our confidence that the subprocess communication is correct.

> Subprocess communication can be operating system-specific, particularly when output redirection is involved. One advantage of Go is that the pipe method we present here works equally well across operating systems, with no extra modification needed, whereas, in other languages such as Python, additional work is sometimes required.

While the code is succinct and easy to debug, the need to start a new Python process to handle every request can impact performance for applications with smaller, quicker models. Furthermore, it creates a fairly tight coupling between the Go application and its Python model. This could pose an issue in larger teams where a data science team creates a model and a software development team creates the rest of the application. It could also create issues where the model should be exposed to multiple applications, not just one – what should you do then? Have one copy of the model for each application? This could lead to maintainability issues. In the following example, we will look at one way to decouple the Go application from its Python model.

Example – invoking a Python model using HTTP

What if the model resides on a different machine, we need to decouple the Go and model logic, or if there are multiple actions we may wish to perform, such as training a user-specific model based on user data, and later use this model to generate a prediction? In those cases, our previous solution using command-line arguments will become more complex as we add more arguments to distinguish between actions and return codes. This type of invocation is generally known as **Remote Procedure Call** (**RPC**), and solutions such as SOAP or JSON-RPC have been known to the industry for decades[7].

In the following example, we will use a more universal and generic protocol: HTTP. Strictly speaking, HTTP is a data transfer protocol, and one that is often used as the plumbing for RPC protocols. However, with very little effort, we can create our own minimal RPC on top of HTTP by exposing a single endpoint that will accept POST requests. This has the advantage that no dependencies beyond the standard library in either Python or Go are required, and that debugging protocol errors are particularly straightforward. The downside is that it requires a bit more work to handle concerns such as serialization.

The request/response process we will follow is illustrated in the following diagram:

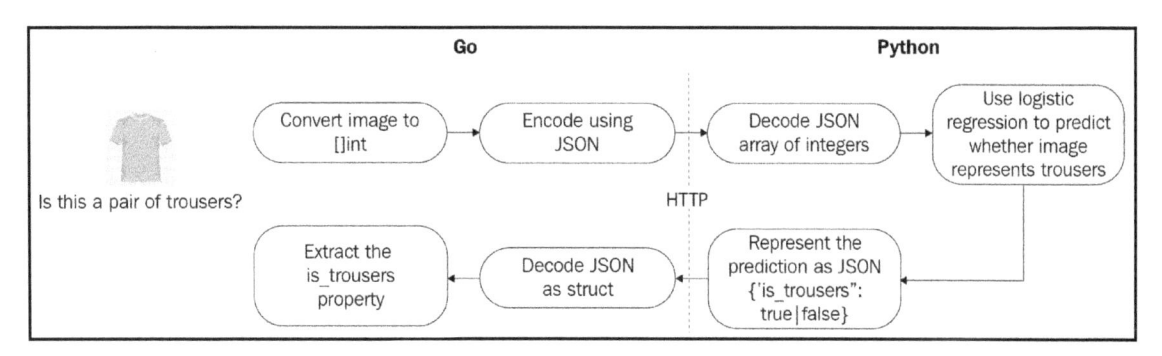

Fig. 2: The request/reply process for a GoML application to communicate with a pretrained Python model using HTTP

Unlike the previous example, we assume that the Python HTTP server is already running. If you are following along with the companion repository, you can start the Python server with the `python3 model_http.py` command after installing its dependencies using `install-python-dependencies.sh`. This means that the Go code is particularly short:

```
// Predict returns whether the ith image represents trousers or not based
on the logistic regression model

func Predict(i int) (bool, error){
    b, err := json.Marshal(testImages[i])
    if err != nil {
        return false, err
    }
    r := bytes.NewReader(b)
    resp, err := http.Post("http://127.0.0.1:8001", "application/json", r)
    if err != nil {
        return false, err
    }
    body, err := ioutil.ReadAll(resp.Body)
    if err != nil {
        return false, err
    }
```

```
        resp.Body.Close()
        var resp struct {
            IsTrousers bool `json:"is_trousers"`
        }
        err := json.Unmarshal(body, &resp)
        return resp.IsTrousers, err
    }
```

As we did previously, we can generate some predictions to ensure communication between Go and Python processes is working as expected:

```
// Expected: true <nil>

Predict(16)
```

As expected, we get back the following:

```
true <nil>
```

We can continue this process for several other images to ensure that the response matches the ground truth value, as defined by the `df.Col("Label")` series. We could also create multiple HTTP endpoints on our Python HTTP server to allow testing of various kinds, further enhancing our confidence in interprocess communication.

> **TIP:** In the likely event that you ever need to debug communication with an HTTP server, a great tool is Postman, a free GUI tool that lets you create HTTP requests and inspect the responses. You can get Postman at: https://www.getpostman.com/.

In the previous examples, we assumed that the model was created in a different programming language (Python) and could only be accessed from that language. However, there are a few popular deep learning libraries that have striven to become more polyglot and, therefore, provide means to create a model using one language and use it using another. In the following examples, we will look at two of these libraries.

Example – deep learning using the TensorFlow API for Go

Deep learning is a subfield of machine learning that employs neural networks, usually with many layers, to solve complex problems such image or speech recognition. In this example, we will look at how to leverage TensorFlow, a popular deep learning framework, using its Go bindings.

TensorFlow is a highly optimized library that was created by Google to perform calculations on objects called tensors[8]. If a vector is a collection of scalar entries (numbers) and a matrix a collection of vectors, then a tensor can be thought of as a higher-dimensional matrix, of which scalars, vectors, and matrices are special cases. While this may seem a bit abstract, tensors are natural objects to use when describing neural networks, and this is why TensorFlow has become one of the most popular libraries—even *the* most popular, according to some commentators—for commercial and academic deep learning development[9][10].

In 2011, the team at Google Brain built a proprietary deep learning system called DistBelief[11]. A number of prominent computer scientists such as Jeff Dean and Geoffrey Hinton worked on its backpropagation and other neural network-related algorithms, leading to an increased uptake of the framework across many projects at Google. In 2017, the second generation of this framework, now called TensorFlow, was released under an open source license[12].

TensorFlow is at its core a low-level API, also known as a backend for deep learning computations. Practically speaking, a data scientist working a commercial problem does not usually need to interact directly with the TensorFlow API on a daily basis. Instead, a number of frontends, such as Keras, which we introduced previously, are available as higher-level abstractions over TensorFlow and offer the best of both the performance and ease-of-use worlds. On the other hand, academic research where new types of neural architectures are invented is often performed using the low-level API, because no abstractions exist for the new constructs yet. The objects you create in TensorFlow, called **graphs**, can be persisted and reused in other languages, thanks to recent efforts to make the framework more polyglot[13].

In this example, we will explain how to install TensorFlow and how to use its Go API to load a pretrained TensorFlow model and use it to make a prediction.

Installing TensorFlow

The TensorFlow experience is usually a slick one—that is, after you have managed to install it correctly. The TensorFlow team recognized that this was a difficult step, and that building TensorFlow from source usually took hours in the best case, and as a result they now provide several easy installation options. It is worth noting that, if you have a compatible GPU on your system, you should install a GPU option as this will usually accelerate the software significantly, something particularly noticeable in the training phase:

- **Install with pip**: TensorFlow is aimed at Python programmers who will typically use `pip` to manage their packages. At the time of writing, this method has been tested with Ubuntu Linux 16.04 or later, macOS 10.12.6 (Sierra) or later (albeit with no GPU support), Raspbian 9.0 or later, and Windows 7 or later.
- **Use a Docker image**: This will work with a wide range of systems that support Docker. There are two images to choose from: a vanilla TensorFlow image and one that also includes Jupyter, allowing you to have the same experience as gophernotes but with Python only.
- **Build from source**: This is best option if you are using a non-standard configuration or want to exert specific control over part of the build process (perhaps take advantage of some optimization that will only work for your particular configuration).

> There is also a fourth option, which is to use Google Colaboratory to run TensorFlow-based code in Google's cloud, but we will not delve into this option, as it currently only works with Python.

In this example, we will use a Docker image. Docker can be seen as a solution for packaging and running multiple applications (called containers) on the same machine while keeping them from interfering with one another. If you are not already familiar with it, head to `https://docs.docker.com/get-started/` for a five-minute tutorial.

We will use the vanilla TensorFlow-on-Ubuntu image called `tensorflow/tensorflow`, which does not include Jupyter. We will need to install Go on top of this image so that we can run our code. Because our code will depend on TensorFlow bindings for Go, we will also install them according to the official instructions[14]. This will require us to install the TensorFlow C bindings, too. Our Dockerfile will thus look as follows. Some steps have been omitted for brevity – you can find the full Dockerfile in the companion repository for this book:

```
FROM tensorflow/tensorflow

## Install gcc for cgo ##
RUN apt-get update && apt-get install -y --no-install-recommends \
 curl \
 git \
 wget \
 g++ \
 gcc \
 libc6-dev \
 make \
 pkg-config \
 && rm -rf /var/lib/apt/lists/*

## Install TensorFlow C library ##
RUN curl -L \
"https://storage.googleapis.com/tensorflow/libtensorflow/libtensorflow-cpu-linux-x86_64-1.13.1.tar.gz" | \
 tar -C "/usr/local" -xz
RUN ldconfig

## Install Go ##
ENV GOLANG_VERSION 1.9.2

RUN wget -O go.tgz
"https://golang.org/dl/go${GOLANG_VERSION}.${goRelArch}.tar.gz"; \
 echo "${goRelSha256} *go.tgz" | sha256sum -c -; \
 tar -C /usr/local -xzf go.tgz; \
 rm go.tgz; \
 \
 if [ "$goRelArch" = 'src' ]; then \
 echo >&2; \
 echo >&2 'error: UNIMPLEMENTED'; \
 echo >&2 'TODO install golang-any from jessie-backports for
GOROOT_BOOTSTRAP (and uninstall after build)'; \
 echo >&2; \
 exit 1; \
 fi; \
 \
```

Using Pretrained Models

```
    export PATH="/usr/local/go/bin:$PATH"; \
    go version

ENV GOPATH /go
ENV PATH $GOPATH/bin:/usr/local/go/bin:$PATH

RUN mkdir -p "$GOPATH/src" "$GOPATH/bin" && chmod -R 777 "$GOPATH"

## Go get tensorflow go library ##
RUN \
 go get github.com/tensorflow/tensorflow/tensorflow/go \
 github.com/tensorflow/tensorflow/tensorflow/go/op

## Set up the environment so we can just run our code ##
RUN mkdir $GOPATH/src/model

WORKDIR $GOPATH/src/model

ADD . $GOPATH/src/model

CMD ["go", "run", "main.go"]
```

Import the pretrained TensorFlow model

In `Chapter 3`, *Supervised Learning*, we explained how to create a deep learning model in pure Go using the go-deep library. While this worked as a toy example, it was quite slow to train and required a lot of superfluous code. It would have been much easier, and resulted in more performance code, to use one of the industry-leading deep learning libraries, but unfortunately they are written in other languages. Using the Python library Keras, we have created a deep learning model that will serve as a classifier in the same problem that we looked at previously: *Is the given image of a pair of trousers?* We will now write some Go code to import our pretrained model.

> **TIP**
> What if only the weights of the model were saved, rather than the more complete SavedModel format? In that case, you can still import it using the `graph.Import` func, but, subsequently, more work is required to tell TensorFlow about all the operations and variables. There is an example in the TensorFlow API godocs that illustrates this process[15].

What follows assumes that the model was saved in the SavedModel format and that we know the names of the input and output Ops. If the model was created by someone else using Keras or another third-party library, this can sometimes be tricky. One option is to use the SavedModel command-line interface tool to inspect the model[16].

> **TIP**
> If the model was created in Keras and you have access to the Python code, just inspect its input and output properties to see the names of the corresponding tensors. They may have a :0 appended to them, which you can ignore.

To restore a SavedModel in Go, simply use the LoadSavedModel func. This will return a Graph and Session object that you can then operate on, passing inputs and retrieving outputs:

```
savedModel, err := tf.LoadSavedModel("./saved_model", []string{"serve"}, nil)
if err != nil {
  log.Fatalf("failed to load model: %v", err)
}
```

Note that the second argument, called the tag, is often set to serve by convention. We can now access the input and output operations:

```
input := savedModel.Graph.Operation("input_input_1")
output := savedModel.Graph.Operation("output_1/BiasAdd")
```

If either the input or output is nil at this stage, this means that you do not have the correct names, so you will need to return to inspecting the model to find out what they should be. It can also be useful to look at savedModel.Graph.Operations, which is a slice of Operation, and filter the list of operations down by those containing the search string input in their Name().

We can now access the restored session and graph:

```
session := savedModel.Session
graph := savedModel.Graph
defer session.Close()
fmt.Println("Successfully imported model!")
```

Now, we can run this code inside our TensorFlow Docker container and see the result. We will build the Docker image from its Dockerfile and run it:

```
docker build -t tfgo . && \
docker run -it tfgo
```

Using Pretrained Models

If everything goes well, we should see some output while the container is being built (this will run much faster the second time) with the following messages at the end:

```
Successfully built 9658a6232ef8
Successfully tagged tfgo:latest
Successfully imported model!
```

The first two lines tell us that our Docker image was successfully built, and the last line comes from our Go code and lets us know that the model import operation worked without resulting in any errors.

> **TIP**: Depending on how you installed Docker, you may need superuser privileges to run these commands, so just prefix them with `sudo` if required.

Creating inputs to the TensorFlow model

Now that we are able to recreate the TensorFlow graph and session from a `SavedModel`, we will create a procedure that will accept an image from the MNIST fashion dataset as a slice of bytes and use these bytes to populate the inputs of the model we loaded previously. Then, we will be able to run the model to get an output prediction.

We must create a procedure that will accept an image from the MNIST fashion dataset and return a tensor of the correct shape. We know from Chapter 3, *Supervised Learning*, that the model will expect a slice of 784 floats, and an inspection of the model (using `model.summary` in Python, or the `SavedModel` CLI) will reveal that the inputs should be a 1 x 784 tensor of `float32` values.

> When constructing tensors by passing slices of slices as an argument to the `NewTensor` func, make sure that they are all the same length. For example, you can pass 3 slices containing 7 elements each, and this will create a (3,7) tensor, but not 3 slices containing 5, 6, and 7 elements, respectively—the second dimension must be the same for all slices.

We can construct a blank (zero) tensor with the right shape like so:

```
func makeBlankInputTensor() (*tf.Tensor, error) {
  t := make([][]float32, 1)
  t[0] = make([]float32, 784)
  tensor, err := tf.NewTensor(t)
  return tensor, err
}
```

While this is not very useful on its own, it illustrates the use of the NewTensor func, which can infer the correct tensor shape and value type from the Go interface{} it is passed. Using the ImageSeriesToFloats func we introduced in Chapter 3, *Supervised Learning*, we can easily convert an image into a slice of float32 and thus make the input tensor.

We can run the model to get a prediction:

```
tensor, err := makeTensorFromImage("/path/to/fashion/MNIST", 12)
if err != nil {
  log.Fatal(err)
}
prediction, err := session.Run(
  map[tf.Output]*tf.Tensor{
    graph.Operation(input.Name()).Output(0): tensor,
  },
  []tf.Output{
    graph.Operation(output.Name()).Output(0),
  },
  nil)
if err != nil {
  log.Fatal(err)
}

probability := prediction[0].Value().([][]float32)[0][0]
if probability > 0.5 {
  fmt.Printf("It's a pair of trousers! Probability: %v\n", probability)
} else {
  fmt.Printf("It's NOT a pair of trousers! Probability: %v\n", probability)
}
```

For example, when running this with a blank tensor as the input, the last few lines of output are as follows:

```
Successfully built b7318b44f92d
Successfully tagged tfgo:latest
Successfully imported model!
It's NOT a pair of trousers! Probability: 0.04055497
```

In the following chapter, we will explore the pattern of using Docker to deploy ML application workloads in more detail.

Summary

In this chapter, we compared Go-only and polyglot ML solutions from a practical point of view, contrasting their drawbacks and advantages. We then presented two generic solutions to develop polyglot ML solutions: the os/exec package and JSON-RPC. Finally, we looked at two highly-specialized libraries that come with their own RPC-based integration solutions: TensorFlow and Caffe. You have learned how to decide whether to use a Go-only or polyglot approach to ML in your application, how to implement an RPC-based polyglot ML application, and how to run TensorFlow models from Go.

In the next chapter, we will cover the last step of the ML development life cycle: taking an ML application written in Go to production.

Further readings

1. *Keras GitHub repository*: `https://github.com/keras-team/keras`. Retrieved April 30, 2019.
2. *GitHub search for keras*: `https://github.com/search?utf8=%E2%9C%93&q=keras&type=`. Retrieved April 30, 2019.
3. *GitHub content search for keras*: `https://github.com/search?q=keras&type=Code`. Retrieved April 30, 2019.
4. *Python is Becoming the World's Most Popular Coding Language*, The Economist. July 26, 2018: `https://www.economist.com/graphic-detail/2018/07/26/python-is-becoming-the-worlds-most-popular-coding-language`. Retrieved April 30, 2019.
5. *Using Python on Unix Platforms*: `https://docs.python.org/2/using/unix.html`. Retrieved April 30, 2019.
6. *JSON*: `https://www.json.org/`. Retrieved April 30, 2019.
7. *Cover Pages – SOAP*: `http://xml.coverpages.org/soap.html`. Retrieved April 30, 2019.
8. *TensorFlow Core*: `https://www.tensorflow.org/overview/`. Retrieved April 30, 2019.
9. *Deep Learning Framework Power Scores*: `https://towardsdatascience.com/deep-learning-framework-power-scores-2018-23607ddf297a`. Retrieved April 30, 2019.

10. *Ranking Popular Deep Learning Frameworks*: https://blog.thedataincubator.com/2017/10/ranking-popular-deep-learning-libraries-for-data-science/. Retrieved April 30, 2019.
11. Dean, Jeff et. al. *Large-Scale Machine Learning on Heterogeneous Distributed Systems*. Nov. 9, 2015. http://download.tensorflow.org/paper/whitepaper2015.pdf. Retrieved April 30, 2019.
12. *TensorFlow* RELEASE.md: https://github.com/tensorflow/tensorflow/blob/07bb8ea2379bd459832b23951fb20ec47f3fdbd4/RELEASE.md. Retrieved April 30, 2019.
13. *TensorFlow in Other Languages*: https://www.tensorflow.org/guide/extend/bindings. Retrieved April 30, 2019.
14. *Installing TensorFlow for Go*: https://www.tensorflow.org/install/lang_go . Retrieved May 1, 2019.
15. *TensorFlow—godocs*: https://godoc.org/github.com/tensorflow/tensorflow/tensorflow/go. Retrieved May 3, 2019.
16. *Save and Restore*: https://www.tensorflow.org/guide/saved_model#install_the_savedmodel_cli. Retrieved May 3, 2019.
17. *Tag constants*: https://github.com/tensorflow/tensorflow/blob/master/tensorflow/python/saved_model/tag_constants.py. Retrieved May 22, 2019.

6
Deploying Machine Learning Applications

In the previous chapters, we learned how to create an application that can prepare data (Chapter 2, *Setting Up the Development Environment*) for either a supervised (Chapter 3, *Supervised Learning*) or unsupervised (Chapter 4, *Unsupervised Learning*) ML algorithm. We also learned how to evaluate and test the output of these algorithms with the added complication that we have incomplete knowledge about the algorithm's inner state and workings, and must therefore treat it as a black box. In Chapter 5, *Using Pre-Trained Models*, we looked at model persistence and how Go applications can leverage models written in other languages. Together, the skills you have learned so far constitute the fundamentals required to successfully prototype ML applications. In this chapter, we will look at how to prepare your prototype for commercial readiness, focusing on aspects specific to ML applications.

In this chapter, you will cover the following topics:

- The continuous delivery feedback loop, including how to test, deploy, and monitor ML applications
- Deployment models for ML applications

The continuous delivery feedback loop

Continuous delivery (**CD**) is the practice of using short feedback loops in the software development life cycle to ensure that the resulting application can be released at any moment in time[1]. While there are alternative approaches to release management, we will only consider this one because creating a meaningful, short—and therefore automated—feedback loop with ML applications presents unique challenges that are not created by alternative methodologies that may not require this degree of automation.

The CD feedback loop consists of the following process:

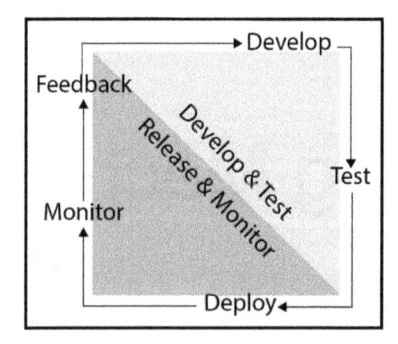

Fig. 1: The continuous delivery feedback loop

Developing

The development portion of the feedback loop is what we have covered so far in this book. As we argued in Chapter 5, *Using Pre-Trained Models*, developing ML models in Go has both advantages and disadvantages, and sometimes combining Go with other languages, such as Python, to benefit from libraries, such as Keras, can significantly shorten the development portion of the cycle. The downside is reduced maintainability and more work to test the resulting solution, as it will necessarily contain a Go–Python interface (for example).

Testing

Because humans are prone to making errors, testing the source code we create is a critical element of the development life cycle to guarantee an accurate and reliable product. Entire books have been dedicated to the subject, and it seems there are as many different approaches to software testing as there are software engineers (as an internet search for software-testing methodologies will confirm). ML applications, on the surface, are particularly difficult to test because they seem like a black box, whose output depends on the training set we provide: we feed them data, and they feed us answers, but a slight change of the train–test split or the hyperparameters could produce a different output for a given input vector. How can we determine whether the answers they provide are erroneous because the model's hyperparameters are incorrect, because the input data is corrupt, or because the model's algorithms are flawed? Or is this particular response an outlier buried in a population of otherwise acceptable responses?

In the previous chapters, we performed statistical testing of models using the validation set to measure the responses of the model to a meaningful sample of inputs, comparing them to expected output values when these were available (supervised learning). Arguably, this is the only way to test ML models for accuracy or precision because retraining them on a different sample of the dataset (or with altered hyperparameters) could produce a different output for the same input, but should not produce statistically inferior results on a large validation set with regards to the same accuracy/precision metrics. In other words, with small changes to the model, we could see large changes to the way it responds to one input vector, but its response should not be too different when tested against a large enough sample of input vectors, such as the validation set.

This has two consequences. First, the way that unit tests are usually constructed, where the developer chooses input values and asserts on the output, could break down with the slightest change to the model. Therefore, it is best not to rely on assertions based on a single response. Rather, it is better to assert using an accuracy or precision metric across a larger set, using the techniques we introduced in `Chapters 3`, *Supervised Learning*, and `Chapter 4`, *Unsupervised Learning*.

Second, there may be edge cases, where we wish to guarantee the behavior of a model, or certain responses that we wish to guarantee will never occur (not even as outlying behavior). If we cannot be sure that a black box model can achieve this, combining an ML algorithm with traditional logic is the only way to ensure that the constraints are met. For example, consider Google's recent ban of "gorilla" as a search term on Google Images in an effort to prevent some accidentally racist results from appearing[2]. Performing statistical testing of the image classifier with gorilla images would have been difficult and would only have covered this one edge case; however, knowing what an unacceptable response was and adding constraining logic to prevent this edge case was a trivial, if embarrassing, affair. As with this example, traditional unit tests can be combined with statistical testing, with the traditional unit tests asserting on the output of the constraints while the statistical tests assert on the model output directly. An holistic strategy for ML testing thus emerges:

1. **Define accuracy/precision goals for the model**: This may not be as simple as coming up with a single accuracy score, as reducing false positives or false negatives may take precedence. For example, a classifier that aims to determine whether a mortgage applicant should get a loan may be required to err on the side of caution, with more false negatives tolerated than false positives, depending on the risk profile of the lender.
2. **Define edge case behavior and codify this into unit tests**: This may require traditional logic to restrict the output of the ML model to ensure that these constraints are met and traditional unit tests to assert on the constrained output of the ML model.

Deployment

Once the ML application has been developed and you have tested it to satisfy yourself that it works as intended, the next step in the CD life cycle is to deploy the software—that is, take steps to ensure that users are able to access it. There are different deployment models, depending on factors such as whether you are intending to run the application on your own hardware or whether you intend to use an **infrastructure-as-a-service** (**IaaS**) or **platform-as-a-service** (**PaaS**) cloud, and we will touch upon these differences in the next section. Here, we will assume that you are either running the application on your own servers or using a virtual infrastructure supplied by an IaaS provider.

ML applications can present unique challenges in deployment that are absent from simpler software, such as an HTTP server that connects to a database:

- Dependency on scientific libraries that require LAPACK or BLAS entails complex installation processes with many steps, and chances for mistakes.
- Dependency on deep-learning libraries, such as TensorFlow, entails dynamic linking to C libraries, again leading to a complex installation process, with many OS and architecture-specific steps, and chances for mistakes.
- Deep learning models may need to run on specialized hardware (for example, servers with GPUs), even for testing
- Where should ML models be persisted? Should they be committed as though they were source code? If so, how can we be sure we are deploying the correct version?

Next, we will present solutions to these challenges and a sample application that embodies these solutions.

Dependencies

Anyone who has tried to build TensorFlow or NumPy from source will sympathize with the saying that *anything that can go wrong, will go wrong*. A search on Google, Stack Overflow, or their respective GitHub issue pages will reveal many obscure potential issues with the build process[3][4][5]. These are not isolated finding in the sense that the scientific computing libraries that ML applications rely on tend to be highly complex and depend on a convoluted set of other libraries that are also highly complex. An academic ML researcher might have need to build dependencies from source to benefit from a certain optimization, or perhaps because they need to modify them. On the contrary, an ML application developer must try to avoid this process and instead use prebuilt images available as Python wheels[6], prebuilt packages for their chosen package manager (such as apt on Ubuntu Linux or Chocolatey[7] on Windows), or Docker images.

We will focus on Docker as a solution for developing and packaging Go ML applications for several reasons:

- Portability across a wide range of operating systems
- Excellent support from major cloud vendors, such as Microsoft Azure[8] and Amazon Web Services[9]
- Support for Docker integration in popular provisioning and infrastructure configuration using tools such as Terraform[10], Chef[11], and Ansible[12].
- Availability of ML libraries through prebuilt Docker images
- Go's particular suitability for Docker, as it can always be configured to produce static binaries, allowing us to greatly reduce the production Docker image size

> **TIP**
> If you have reduced the size of the Docker image as much as possible (maybe by using the `scratch` image), but the size of the Go binary makes the overall image still too large for you, consider using the `strip` command or a packer like `upx`.

In all the examples we have looked at so far, we have created a single Docker image that contains all the dependencies for our application, as well as the application files, usually added to the container using the `ADD` or `COPY` command in the Dockerfile. While this has the advantage of simplicity (there is only one Dockerfile for development and production), it also means that we will need to push or pull an oversized Docker image with all the dependencies for developing an application.

However, the dependencies are probably not required to run it because Go can always be configured to produce static binaries that run on stripped-down Docker images. This means slower deployment times and slower testing times, as intermediate Docker images may not be cached in the CI environment, not to mention that a smaller container tends to use less disk and memory on its host server. Smaller images also have the benefit of added security from reducing the attack surface, as they will contain far fewer dependencies that an attacker could exploit. The `scratch` image, for example, does not even contain a shell, making it very hard for an attacker to compromise, even if the application running in the container is itself compromised.

The process we advocate is shown in the following diagram:

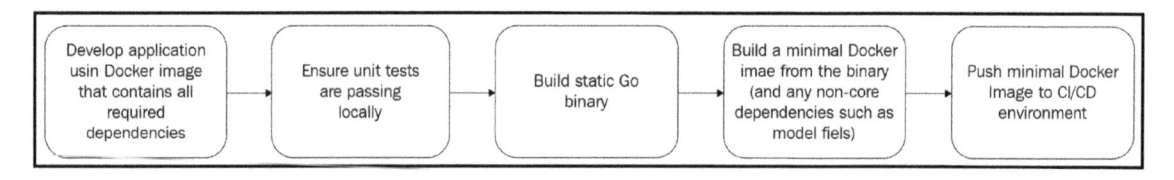

Develop application usin Docker image that contains all required dependencies → Ensure unit tests are passing locally → Build static Go binary → Build a minimal Docker imae from the binary (and any non-core dependencies such as model fiels) → Push minimal Docker Image to CI/CD environment

Fig 2: Deployment using two separate Docker images (one for development and one for testing/production)

In the following example, we assume that you already have a development environment, where all your dependencies live (which could be Docker based, or not—it does not matter). You have developed your ML application, which consists of a `main` package and some saved model weights, `model.data`, and would like to create a production-ready container. To create this container, we need to do two things.

First, we need to compile the Go application to a static binary. If you are not using CGO and linking to some C libraries (such as the TensorFlow C library), then using `go build` without any additional flags will suffice. However, if your application depends on, say, the TensorFlow C library, then you need to add some additional command-line arguments to ensure that the resulting binary is static—that is, that it includes all the dependent code. At the time of writing, there is a proposal for Go 1.13 to have a `-static` flag for the `build` command that will achieve this with no further work. Until then, there is an excellent blog post by Diogok that explains the different flags in the following command, and how to tweak them if it does not work in your particular case:

```
CGO_ENABLED=0 GOOS=linux GOARCH=amd64 go build -a -tags netgo -ldflags '-w -extldflags "-static"' -o mlapp *.go
```

This will produce a single output binary `mlapp` with all the required dependencies. The purpose of using all these flags is to produce a static binary that contains all our dependencies so that we only have the simple task of adding them to a "vanilla" Docker image, giving us the Dockerfile:

```
FROM scratch
ADD . /usr/share/app
ENTRYPOINT ["/usr/share/app/mlapp"]
```

That's it! There is nothing else to add, unlike the long Dockerfiles we previously used because we needed all the dependencies. In this case, we already have these dependencies inside our Go binary. This is another advantage of Go; unlike some other programming languages, Go makes this type of deployment possible.

> **TIP:** You can also expose a port using your Dockerfile (for example, if you intend to serve your app from an HTTP server) by using the `EXPOSE` command. To expose an HTTP server listening on port 80, use the, `EXPOSE 80/tcp` command.

In the preceding example, we assumed that our model file containing the trained model weights/hyperparameters was persisted to disk and saved alongside our binary, ready to be added to the Docker container; however, there are cases where this may be impractical or undesirable.

Model persistence

Most of the time, you can follow the aforementioned pattern of committing your model file alongside the source code and adding it to a Docker image during deployment together with your binary; however, there are times when you may want to reconsider this:

- The model file is very large, so it leads to a very large Docker image and slows down deployments.
- The number of model files you have is dynamic and each model is associated with an object of your application—that is, you train one model per user.
- The model is retrained much more frequently than the code is likely to change, leading to very frequent deployments.

In these cases, you may want to make the model available from a different source and not commit it to source control. At a basic level, model files are just a sequence of bytes, so there is no real limit to where they can be stored: on a file server elsewhere, cloud file storage, or a database.

The exception is the second case: where you have a dynamic number of model files that are associated with application objects, such as users. For example, if you are building a system that aims to forecast how much electricity a household will consume the following day, you might end up having one model for all households or one model per household. In the latter case, you would be better served using a database to hold these model files:

- The model files could be seen to contain sensitive data that is probably best secured and governed in a database.
- A large number of model files could benefit from advanced compression techniques that are leveraged by database software, such as using page-level compression instead of row-level compression. This can reduce their overall size on the disk.

- It may be easier to keep data associated with application objects all in the same place to limit the number of queries required with authorize an operation related to a model, for example.

For these reasons, among others, we recommend saving the model to a database in the event that your application requires many models, each associated to an application object, such as a user.

This poses a small challenge, because some Go ML libraries, such as GoML, expose persistence functions, such as `PersistToFile` of the `linear` package models, and these functions persist the model to a file; however, they do not directly offer access to serialized model should we want to persist it elsewhere.

There are two techniques we can apply:

- Look through the Godocs to see if the model struct has any unexported fields. If not, we can simply use `encoding/json` to serialize the model.
- If there are unexported fields, we can save the model to a temporary file, read the temporary file into memory, and delete it again.

> In Go, an **unexported field** is a struct field with a lowercase name, which is not accessible outside the package in which it is defined. Such fields are absent from serialization using `encoding/json`.

In the case of GoML's `LeastSquares` model, there are no unexported fields, and a cursory examination of the `PersistToFile` method would reveals that it is using encoding/JSON to marshal the model to a byte slice. Therefore, we can just use `serializedModel, err := json.Marshal(leastSquaresModel)` to serialize it. The resulting `serializedModel` can then be saved anywhere we wish.

But what if, for argument's sake, we could not do this because the model struct had unexported fields? For example, the golearn library's `linear_models` package has an `Export` method that persists models to the file, but this relies on a call to a C function, and the model has unexported fields. In this case, we have no choice but to first persist the model to a temporary file and then recover the file contents:

```go
import (
  "io/ioutil"
  linear "github.com/sjwhitworth/golearn/linear_models"
)

func Marshal(model *linear.Model) ([]byte, error) {
  tmpfile, err := ioutil.TempFile("", "models")
```

```
    if err != nil {
      return nil, err
    }
    defer os.Remove(tmpfile.Name())
    if err := linear.Export(model, tmpfile.Name()); err != nil {
      return nil, err
    }
    return ioutil.ReadAll(tmpfile)
}
```

All we are doing in the preceding code is providing a temporary location to store the model file on disk and then moving it back to memory. While this is not the most performant way to store a model, it is necessary because of the limitations on some of the interfaces for some Go ML libraries, and there is already an open issue on GoLearn's GitHub page to improve this.

Now that the application is deployed, we want some certainty that it is functioning correctly, using up an appropriate amount of resources, and that there is no underlying issue that could prevent it from being available. In the next subsection, we will look at monitoring techniques specific to ML applications.

Monitoring

In his book, *Architecting for Scale*, Lee Atchison, Principal Cloud Architect at New Relic, argues for the use of a risk matrix, also known as a **risk register**, to keep track of what is likely to go wrong with an application and how it should be mitigated[16]. While this may seem like overkill for a simple application, it is a great tool for managing risk in a complex environment, especially where ML models are involved. This is because the entire team can be aware of the main risks, their likelihoods, and mitigation, even if they did not have a hand in creating every part of the application in the first place. ML models can sometimes be created by a data scientist and then later handed over to a software development team via one of the polyglot integration approaches we outlined in Chapter 5, *Supervised Learning*, so this makes knowing any risk associated with their use in production all the more important.

While this may seem like a rather opinionated approach, remember that the goal is simply to make developers think about what can cause their application to become unavailable. There is no obligation to write down a risk register or run your team using one (although both could be beneficial), and the practice of thinking about risk always helps by shining light on dark recesses, where no one had thought to look for that elusive Friday night bug that took the whole application offline until Monday morning.

> A **risk** associated with a production application is different from a failure of a test, which you would hopefully have caught before deploying it to production in the first place. It is the risk that something you assumed constant in testing (such as available memory or a training algorithm converging) has changed to a critical state.

Risks associated with ML applications could include, but are not limited to, the following:

- Running out of memory to run more instances of the model
- A model file becoming corrupt, leading to the model being unavailable to be run, even though the rest of the application might still be available
- A nonconvergent training procedure, if model retraining is done in production, leading to a useless model
- Malicious users crafting input to try to trick the model into producing a desired output
- Malicious users crafting badly formatted input (fuzzing) to crash the model
- Upstream services, such as databases used to store ML models, being unavailable
- The cloud datacentre, where the model runs runs low on GPU availability, meaning that an autoscale feature fails and availability of your deep learning model is reduced as a result

The list is obviously not exhaustive, but hopefully it gives you an idea of the kind of issues that could arise so you can look for them in your own applications. Because it is very difficult to come up with an exhaustive list, general monitoring principles apply:

- Use structured logging in the application wherever possible and centralize these logs
- If retraining in production, make sure that you set up alerts for any error in the training procedure, since this will necessarily lead to a useless model (or falling back to a deprecated one)
- Capture metrics whose significant change could be used to detect any risks in your register materializing (for example, availability of memory space)

Go was designed partly to serve web applications[17], so there are many third-party packages that can help you perform these tasks, and we will now explore some of them.

Structured logging

There are many logging libraries for Go, such as the standard library's `log` package[18][19][20]. A significant advantage to using a structured logging library—which logs to a standardized format, such as JSON—over unstructured logging that simply uses free text is that it is far easier to work with the log data once it has been created. Not only is searching by a particular field easier (using, say, `jq`[21] to work with JSON data), but structured logs allow far richer integration with existing monitoring and analytics tooling, such as Splunk[22] or Datadog[23].

In the following example, we will use the Logrus package to log an error message returned by a training procedure. Note that the use of this particular logging package is a personal choice, and any other structured logging package would also work.

First, we configure the logger:

```
import "github.com/sirupsen/logrus"

logrus.SetFormatter(&logrus.JSONFormatter{})
logrus.SetReportCaller(true) // Add a field that reports the func name
```

The output format can be configured by using the properties of the `JSONFormatter` struct[24]:

- `TimestampFormat`: The format of the timestamps using a time-compatible format string (for example, `Mon Jan 2 15:04:05 -0700 MST 2006`).
- `DisableTimestamp`: Removes the timestamp from the output
- `DataKey`: Instead of a flat JSON output, this puts all the log entry parameters into a map at the given key
- `FieldMap`: Use this to rename the default output properties, such as the timestamp
- `CallerPrettyfier`: When `ReportCaller` is activated (as shown in the preceding code snippet), this function can be called to customize the output—for example, stripping the package name from the caller's method
- `PrettyPrint`: This determines whether to indent JSON output

Here is an example, where we use it in practice:

```
import "github.com/sajari/regression"
model := new(regression.Regression)
 logrus.WithFields(logrus.Fields{ "model": "linear regression",
}).Info("Starting training")
for i := range trainingX {
```

```
    model.Train(regression.DataPoint(trainingY[i], trainingX[i]))
  }
  if err := model.Run(); err != nil {

  logrus.WithFields(log.Fields{
    "model": "linear regression",
    "error": err.Error(), }).Error("Training error")

  }
    logrus.WithFields(logrus.Fields{ "model": "linear regression",
  }).Info("Finished training")
```

While this may produce more output than necessary, because of the addition of the two info-level messages, we can filter out this level of output if it is not required by using `logrus.SetLevel`; however, in the case of retraining in production, the training time is important (as is making sure that the training process completes), so it is never a bad idea to have records of the process in the log, even if it becomes more verbose as a result.

> **TIP**
> When logging ML-related information, it is a good idea to have a field with the model name (which may be something meaningful to a data scientist, if they created it). When you have multiple models running concurrently in production, it is sometimes hard to tell which one has produced the error!

The time taken to train an algorithm is one metric that we would recommend computing regularly and sending to a dedicated metrics system. We will discuss capturing metrics in the next subsection.

Capturing metrics

In the preceding example, we inserted info-level messages in the logs to signify the start and end of the training process. While we could look at the timestamp fields of both messages and compare them to determine how long the training process took (Splunk, for example, is able to do this with the right query), a more direct and less cumbersome way to achieve the same result is to monitor this specific datapoint, or metric, explicitly. We could then raise alerts if the training process becomes too long or have a chart that logs and displays the time taken by the regular model training processes.

There are two approaches that we can use:

- Store the metric as an additional field on the log entry with a `float64` value
- Store the metric in a separate analytics system

Ultimately, the approach you take depends on your current analytics systems, team preferences, and application size. As far as ML applications go, either approach works equally well, so we will assume the first one, as it reduces the amount of third-party application code required.

Reusing the same example as earlier, let's set this up:

```
import "github.com/sajari/regression"
model := new(regression.Regression)
 log.WithFields(log.Fields{ "model": "linear regression", }).Info("Starting training")
start := time.Now()

for i := range trainingX {
 model.Train(regression.DataPoint(trainingY[i], trainingX[i]))
}
if err := model.Run(); err != nil {
log.WithFields(log.Fields{ "model": "linear regression",
 "error": err.Error(), }).Error("Training error")

}
elapsed := time.Since(start)
 log.WithFields(log.Fields{ "model": "linear regression",
 "time_taken": elapsed.Seconds(), }).Info("Finished training")
```

Note that we did not include any of the logging calls in the timed block. This is because we want to measure the time taken by the training process rather than any logging around it.

> **TIP**
> If your company uses an analytics system, such as Grafana or InfluxDB, you can still use the same approach as previously described—just make sure that you create a sensible name for your metric, including the name of the ML model.

In the final subsection the CD feedback loop, we will consider how accuracy/precision metrics can help create a feedback loop in an ML application.

Feedback

The process of acquiring feedback in any system is intended to improve the system. In the case of an ML application, feedback can help make the application more robust with regards to risks on its register (or the addition of new risks that were previously unmitigated), but this is not specific to ML applications; all production applications benefit from a feedback cycle. There is, however, one special feedback cycle that is particular to ML applications.

An ML model is used on the basis that it satisfies some accuracy/precision criteria that make it better or more generic at extracting meaning from data than a naive heuristic. In `Chapter 3`, *Supervised Learning*, and `Chapter 4`, *Unsupervised Learning*, we outlined some of these metrics, such as the mean square error of a regression of house prices or the test/validation accuracy of binary classifiers on images of clothes. In our CD cycle so far, we have assumed that once a model is created, its accuracy will never change with regards to new input; however, this is rarely a realistic assumption.

Consider our MNIST fashion classifier from `Chapter 3`, *Supervised Learning*, which aims to determine whether an image represents a pair of trousers or not. At the moment, this database does not contain any images of flared trousers. What if these come back into fashion and all the images our model begins to receive are of flared trousers? We may notice users complaining that images are not being correctly classified. Such considerations have led to numerous websites that rely on ML models adding "Rate my prediction" models to their websites in a bid to ensure that models are still outputting relevant predictions.

This is, of course, a valid approach, albeit one that relies on the customer to tell you when your product is and is not working. Because customers are more likely to use these feedback features during an unsatisfactory experience[26], any data you gather from this exercise, while still useful, is likely biased toward the negative and therefore cannot automatically be used as a proxy accuracy metric.

In cases where the customer supplies images and your model classifies them, this may still be your best option, unless you can write a scraper for new trouser images that continuously feeds them to a model and measures its response. That would be labor-intensive, but would clearly produce better results, assuming, of course, that the types of trousers found by your scraper were representative of the types of trouser images supplied by your customers. In other cases, some automated feedback loops may be possible, where you are able to directly monitor the accuracy of a model, either in testing or production, and use this to make a decision on when the model should be retrained.

Consider a different scenario, one where you are asked to forecast the next day's individual electricity consumption of a large number of households, given data points such as the number of occupants and a forecast temperature curve. You decide that you will use, say, one regression per household and store the regression parameters in a database once the model is trained. Then, every day, you will run every model in your database to generate predictions.

A very easy feedback cycle exists in this case because, every day, you can also measure the actual electricity consumption of the household and compare this to your model's prediction. A scheduled script could then compare the relative difference between the two over a certain period, perhaps using a moving average to smooth out any anomalies, and should this difference be greater than a certain predefined threshold, it would then be entitled to assume that some of the model's input data had changed and the model required retraining on a new dataset. An alternative would be to retrain that the model if any of its input parameters changed, although that could lead to a lot of unnecessary retraining and thus additional cost, as forecast temperature curves likely change daily, so every model would likely need to be re-trained every day.

The feedback loop for ML applications with continuous validation and retraining is as follows:

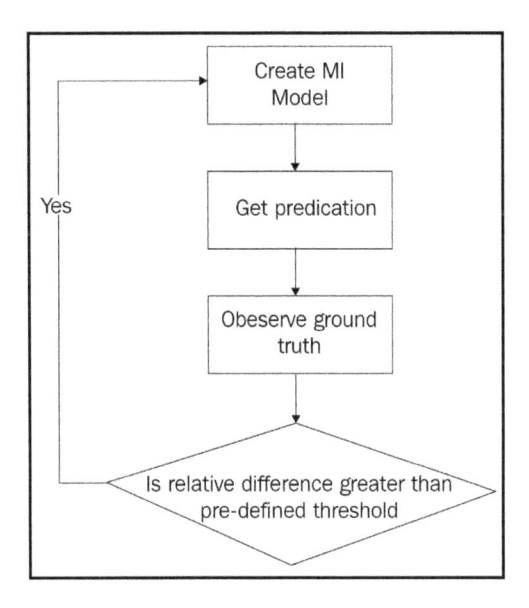

Fig. 3: The feedback loop for ML applications with continuous validation

> **TIP:** The feedback loop cannot be applied to every ML application, but with a little creativity, you can usually find a way in which to find input samples that were not in either the training or testing dataset, but are of updated relevance. If you can automate the process of generating predictions from these samples and storing their difference to a ground truth, then you can still generate the same feedback loop.

Deployment models for ML applications

In the preceding example, we explained how to deploy an ML application using Docker to encompass it and its dependencies. We deliberately stayed away from any discussion pertaining to the infrastructure that was going to run these containers or any Platform-as-a-Service offerings that could facilitate the development or deployment itself. In the current section, we consider different deployment models for ML applications under the assumption that the application will be deployed to a cloud platform that supports both IAAS and platform-as-a-service models, such as Microsoft Azure and Amazon Web Services.

> This section is specifically written to help you decide what virtual infrastructure to use if you are deploying an ML application to the cloud.

There are two main deployment models for any cloud application:

- **Infrastructure-as-a-service**: This is the cloud service that offers a high-level interaction with virtualized hardware, such as virtual machines, without the customer needing to maintain the hardware or the virtualization layer.
- **Platform-as-a-service**: This is a cloud service that offers Software-as-a-Service components that you can then build your application from, such as a serverless execution environment (for example, AWS Lambda).

We will consider both options and how to make best use of them for ML applications. We will compare and contrast the three main vendors by market share, as of Q4 2018: Amazon Web Services, Microsoft Azure, and Google Cloud[30].

Infrastructure-as-a-service

Earlier in this chapter, we explained how to package an ML application using Docker. In this subsection, we will look at simple ways to deploy an ML application using Docker to AWS, Azure, or Google Cloud.

In each case, we will start by explaining how to push one of your local Docker images to a **registry** (that is, a machine that will store images and serve them to the rest of your infrastructure). There are several advantages to using a Docker registry to store your images:

- **Faster deployments and build times**: Virtual infrastructure components requiring images can just pull them from the registry instead of building them from scratch every time
- **Ease of implementing autoscale in your application**: If you have to wait for a long Docker build—say, 20 minutes, for TensorFlow—every time you need to scale your service up, you may experience degradation or unavailability
- **Security**: Pulling images from a single trusted source reduces the attack surface

Amazon Web Services

The core of AWS's virtualized IaaS offering is **Elastic Compute** (**EC2**). AWS also offers **Elastic Container Registry** (**ECR**) as a registry service to serve images from. To set this up, go through the following steps:

> Before you can push or pull an image to an ECR registry, you need `ecr:GetAuthorizationToken` permissions.

1. Tag your image, assuming its ID is `f8ab2d331c34`:

   ```
   docker tag f8ab2d331c34
   your_aws_account_id.dkr.ecr.region.amazonaws.com/my-ml-app
   ```

2. Push the image to the ECR:

   ```
   docker push your_aws_account_id.dkr.ecr.region.amazonaws.com/my-ml-app
   ```

The image is now available to use from an EC2 instance. First, SSH into your instance where you have installed Docker, following the instructions in Chapter 5, *Using Pre-Trained Models*, and then run the following commands to install Docker and start a container from the image (amend the `docker run` command to add exposed ports or volumes):

```
docker pull your_aws_account_id.dkr.ecr.region.amazonaws.com/my-ml-app && \
docker run -d your_aws_account_id.dkr.ecr.region.amazonaws.com/my-ml-app
```

Microsoft Azure

Similar to Amazon's ECR, which we discussed in the previous subsection, Microsoft Azure offers a registry, Azure Container Registry. We can use this by following the same steps as AWS ECR, but there is a difference, namely the requirement to log in via the Docker command-line interface. Once this is done, you can follow the same instructions as the previous subsection, but with your registry and image details:

```
docker login myregistry.azurecr.io
```

Microsoft also allows Docker as a deployment method for App Service Apps, a managed web app service based on Microsoft's **Internet Information Services** (**IIS**). If you have followed the preceding steps to deploy your Docker image to a registry, you can use the `az` command-line tool to create a web app from your image:

```
az webapp create --resource-group myResourceGroup --plan myAppServicePlan --name <app name> --deployment-container-image-name myregistry.azurecr.io/my-ml-app
```

Google Cloud

Like Amazon and Microsoft, Google also offers a registry, called Container Registry, which can be used as a Docker registry. The steps to use it are the same as for Amazon ECR, except for the addition of a preliminary authentication step using the `gcloud` command-line tool:

```
gcloud auth configure-docker
```

Now you can push the image:

```
docker tag quickstart-image gcr.io/[PROJECT-ID]/quickstart-image:tag1
```

The steps to run a Docker container on a Google Cloud VM are the same as for an EC2 VM, with the addition of the authentication step.

Platform-as-a-Service

With the rising popularity of ML components in applications, cloud vendors have scrambled to provide platform-as-a-service offerings that make it easier to deploy ML applications in an effort to win over customers. It is worth a brief review of each of the three main cloud vendors by market share as of 2018[30]. This is not an attempt to recommend one vendor over another, but rather an attempt to explore solutions while remaining agnostic to any decisions regarding cloud vendors that you may have already made. In other words, the deployment models we will discuss will work in all three clouds—and probably others—but some platforms offer specific services that may better suit certain applications or reduce their development effort.

> Cloud vendors make such frequent changes to their offerings that it is possible that by the time you are reading this, there will be newer, better services than the ones described here. Look in the *Further reading* section for some links to Google Cloud, AWS, and Azure ML services[27][28][29].

Amazon Web Services

Amazon Web Services (**AWS**) has two main types of service offerings regarding ML space:

- **AWS Sagemaker**: A hosted environment to run ML notebooks and SDK to efficiently perform various ML-related tasks, including data labeling
- **AWS AI Services**: A set of pretrained models for specific tasks, such as image recognition

Amazon Sagemaker

Amazon Sagemaker uses Jupyter as a development environment for ML models, as we have done throughout the book. The environment in which these Jupyter notebooks run comes with some Python ML libraries. For Python developers, this service can be thought of as another environment to run ML code with some features to accelerate large-scale learning through AWS resources. An example using Sagemaker to perform hyperparameter tuning on a natural language processing task can be found on the AWS GitHub[31], and for a longer introduction there are some exploratory videos available on YouTube[33]. Unfortunately, at this time, there is no way to use Sagemaker with a Go kernel for Jupyter (such as gophernotes), so it is not a pure-Go solution for interactively developing ML applications in a remote environment.

For Go developers who need to interact with an existing Sagemaker solution, there is an SDK that has much of the same features as the Python SDK[32], so it is possible to use gophernotes locally to create Sagemaker tasks. In fact, the SDK is so powerful that it allows Go developers to access a useful data preprocessing service: the Sagemaker Labeling Job service. This service integrates with Mechanical Turk to provide ground truth labels for training data where they are either missing entirely or from part of the dataset. This saves a lot of time compared to manually setting up Mechanical Turk jobs. The function that exposes this functionality is `CreateLabelingJob`.

> **TIP**: If you need to use a supervised learning algorithm, but have only an unlabeled dataset, consider using Sagemaker's interface to Mechanical Turk to label your dataset cheaply. Alternatively, you can create a labeling task through the Mechanical Turk UI at https://www.mturk.com/.

Amazon AI Services

If there is already a model exposed that solves your ML problem, then there is no need for you to reinvent the wheel and train a new model, especially considering the large resources that AWS will have invested in ensuring the accuracy and efficiency of its models. At the time of writing, the following types of algorithms are available on a pay-for-usage basis:

- **Amazon Personalize**: Built on the same recommendation techniques used by Amazon in their online retail store, these allow you to solve problems, such as showing customers items similar to those they have already bought
- **Amazon Forecast**: Timeseries forecasting models
- **Amazon Rekognition**: Image and video analysis
- **Amazon Comprehend**: Natural language processing tasks and text analysis
- **Amazon Textract**: Large-scale document analysis
- **Amazon Polly**: Text-to-speech
- **Amazon Lex**: Build chatbots in a UI environment
- **Amazon Translate**: Automated translation to and from a multitude of languages
- **Amazon Transcribe**: Speech-to-text service

While none of these services are Go specific, they all offer Go SDKs that you can use to interact with them. This is very similar to the example we saw in `Chapter 5`, *Using Pre-Trained Models*, where a model was exposed over HTTP and we used this protocol to send it data and receive predictions.

Generally, the methods are synchronous—that is, you will get the result in the output argument, and do not need to make a further request later. They also have the same type of signature, where the name of the prediction method may vary, and the structure of the input/output will also vary:

```
func (c *NameOfService) NameOfPredictionMethod(input
    *PredictionMethodInput) (*PredictionMethodOutput, error)
```

By way of example, consider Rekognition, which, like the other services, has a Go SDK[34]. Suppose that we wish to detect faces in an image. For this, we use the `DetectFaces` func; this has the following signature:

```
func (c *Rekognition) DetectFaces(input *DetectFacesInput
    (*DetectFacesOutput, error)
```

The input, in this case, contains, among other things, an array of facial attributes that we wish to be returned, as well as an image, either as base-64 encoded bytes or an S3 object. The output will contain a `FaceDetail` struct, which, among other things, will describe an age range for each face, whether it is bearded, a confidence in its bounding box, any detected emotions, whether they are wearing glasses, and so on. This depends on which facial attributes we requested in the input, and necessarily, the more attributes we requested, the more expensive the request will be (as Amazon will need to run more models to give us the answer).

Generally, if it is possible to build your ML application by composing prebuilt models exposed over SDKs, such as AWS, then you will save a lot of time, and it will allow you to focus on adding value specific to your business; however, there are risks associated with vendor lock-in, and at the time of writing, no other cloud platform offers a feature-for-feature alternative to Amazon AI services.

Microsoft Azure

Azure's main offerings geared at ML applications are as follows:

- **Azure ML Studio**: A UI environment to build ML pipelines and train models
- **Azure Cognitive Services**: Pretrained models exposed over HTTP

Azure ML Studio

Azure ML Studio is a cloud-based IDE for ML. It allows users to import data from other Azure services (such as Blob Storage), transform the data, and use it to train one of the included ML algorithms. The resulting model can then be exposed via HTTP or composed with other Azure services, such as Azure Stream Analytics for a real-time ML application[35].

While it is possible to run custom Python code within the Azure ML Studio UI, at the time of writing, this does not extend to Go; however, because it is possible to expose models via HTTP, you can integrate with an existing Azure ML Studio model by following the same pattern that we discussed in `Chapter 5`, *Using Pretrained Models*, where the `net/http` client is used to make requests. It is worth using the Azure SDK just to generate authentication tokens rather than trying to implement this yourself, as the procedure can be error prone[36]. The JSON structure of the request and response are very simple compared to AWS, so the resulting code can be clean and easy to maintain.

Azure Cognitive Services

Azure Cognitive Services exposes several pretrained ML models over HTTP:

- **Computer Vision**: Image recognition
- **Speech**: Speech recognition and transcription
- **LUIS**: Textual intent analysis
- **Bing Image Search**: Retrieves images matching a text string
- **Bing Web Search**: Retrieves URLs matching a text string
- **Text Analytics**: Sentiment analysis

At the time of writing, there is no Go SDK to interact with Cognitive Services, but it is possible to invoke the models by using the REST API, and Microsoft provides an example of this in a Quickstart article[37].

Google Cloud

Google Cloud currently has two main services to offer ML application developers, in addition to the free Google Colaboratory[29]:

- **AI Platform**: Hosted development environment using Notebooks, VM images, or Kubernetes images
- **AI Hub**: Hosted repository of plug-and-play AI components
- **AI Building Blocks**: Pretrained models, exposed via SDK or HTTP

Because AI Hub is targeted only at Python developers and its deployment model is the same as AI Platform, we will not discuss it any further.

AI Platform

Google's AI Hub is a code-based environment aimed at facilitating all aspects of the ML application development life cycle, from data ingestion to deployment, via AI Platform Prediction (applicable to TensorFlow models exported as a `SavedModel`, as in our Chapter 5, *Using Pretrained Models*, example) or Kubernetes. It has loose integrations with other Google Cloud Services, but remains, at its core, a hosted notebook environment.

Because there is no high-level API to create TensorFlow graphs in Go, analogous to Keras in Python, it is unlikely that a Go developer will find the end-to-end platform useful. However, if you are interacting with a TensorFlow model, using AI Platform Prediction to manage the resources for the model and calling it via HTTP[40] is an excellent strategy, particularly as the model can be made to run on VMs with a Tensor Processing Unit, which can be a significantly cheaper way to run TensorFlow workflows[39].

AI Building Blocks

Google's AI Building Blocks are a suite of pretrained models, exposed via HTTP or through one of Google Cloud's SDKs:

- **Sight**: Includes Vision, for image recognition, and Video, for content discovery
- **Language**: Comprises translation and natural language processing functionality
- **Conversation**: Consists of a speech-to-text model, a text-to-speech model, and a chatbox builder
- **Structured data**:

    - **Recommendations AI**: Recommendation engine
    - **AutoML Tables**: UI to generate predictive models
    - **Cloud Inference AI**: Time series inference and correlations tool

The Go SDK is very easy to use, as the following example shows. The example uses the text-to-speech API to download a recording of the phrase `hello, world`, as spoken by the ML model:

```
package main
import (
    "context"
    "fmt"
```

```go
        "io/ioutil"
        "log"
    texttospeech "cloud.google.com/go/texttospeech/apiv1"
    texttospeechpb
"google.golang.org/genproto/googleapis/cloud/texttospeech/v1"
)
func main() {
    ctx := context.Background()
    c, err := texttospeech.NewClient(ctx)
    if err != nil {
        log.Fatal(err)
    }

    req := texttospeechpb.SynthesizeSpeechRequest{
        Input: &texttospeechpb.SynthesisInput{
        InputSource: &texttospeechpb.SynthesisInput_Text{Text: "Hello, World!"},
    },
    Voice: &texttospeechpb.VoiceSelectionParams{
        LanguageCode: "en-US",
        SsmlGender: texttospeechpb.SsmlVoiceGender_NEUTRAL,
    },
    AudioConfig: &texttospeechpb.AudioConfig{
        AudioEncoding: texttospeechpb.AudioEncoding_WAV,
    },
}
    resp, err := c.SynthesizeSpeech(ctx, &req)
        if err != nil {
        log.Fatal(err)
    }
    filename := "prediction.wav"
    err = ioutil.WriteFile(filename, resp.AudioContent, 0666)
    if err != nil {
        log.Fatal(err)
    }
}
```

As with other models-over-HTTP type services, if you can build your application by composing these premade models, then you can dedicate your time to work on value-adding business logic; however, always consider the downsides of vendor lock-in.

Summary

In this chapter, we discussed how to take a prototype ML application to production. Along the way, we explored concerns that a software developer or DevOps engineer would typically think of, but from an ML application developers point of view. Specifically, we learned how to apply a continuous development life cycle to an ML application and the different ways to deploy ML applications in the cloud.

In the next and final chapter, we will take a step back and look at ML development from a project management point of view.

Further readings

1. *Continuous Software Engineering and Beyond: Trends and Challenges Brian Fitzgerald*, 1st International Workshop on Rapid Continuous Software Engineering. New York, NY: Association for Computing Machinery, pp. 1–9.
2. *Google's solution to accidental algorithmic racism*: ban gorillas: `https://www.theguardian.com/technology/2018/jan/12/google-racism-ban-gorilla-black-people`. Retrieved May 3, 2019.
3. *Building Numpy from source*: `http://robpatro.com/blog/?p=47`. Retrieved May 5, 2019.
4. *Python—Compiling Numpy with OpenBLAS integration*: `https://stackoverflow.com/questions/11443302/compiling-numpy-with-openblas-integration`. Retrieved May 5, 2019.
5. *Issues—TensorFlow*: `https://github.com/tensorflow/tensorflow/issues`. Retrieved May 5, 2019.
6. *Python Wheels*: `https://pythonwheels.com/`. Retrieved May 5, 2019.
7. *Chocolateay—The Package Manager for Windows*: `https://chocolatey.org/`. Retrieved May 5, 2019.
8. *Docker Deployment on Azure*: `https://azure.microsoft.com/en-gb/services/kubernetes-service/docker/`. Retrieved May 5, 2019.
9. *What is Docker? | AWS*: `https://aws.amazon.com/docker/`. Retrieved May 5, 2019.
10. *Docker Provider for Terraform*: `https://www.terraform.io/docs/providers/docker/r/container.html`. Retrieved May 5, 2019.
11. *Chef Cookbook for Docker*: `https://github.com/chef-cookbooks/docker`. Retrieved May 5, 2019.

12. *Docker—manage Docker containers*: `https://docs.ansible.com/ansible/2.6/modules/docker_module.html`. Retrieved May 5, 2019.
13. *cmd/go: build: add static flag:* `https://github.com/golang/go/issues/26492`. Retrieved May 5, 2019.
14. *On Golang static binaries, cross-compiling, and plugins*: `https://medium.com/@diogok/on-golang-static-binaries-cross-compiling-and-plugins-1aed33499671`. Retrieved May 5, 2019.
15. *Saving model outside filesystem*: `https://github.com/sjwhitworth/golearn/issues/220`. Retrieved May 6, 2019.
16. *Architecting for Scale*, Lee Atchison, 2016, O'Reilly Press.
17. *Server-side I/O: Node.js vs PHP vs Java vs Go*: `https://www.toptal.com/back-end/server-side-io-performance-node-php-java-go`. Retrieved May 6, 2019.
18. *Zap*: `https://github.com/uber-go/zap`. Retrieved May 6, 2019.
19. *Logrus*: `https://github.com/sirupsen/logrus`. Retrieved May 6, 2019.
20. *Log*: `https://github.com/apex/log`. Retrieved May 6, 2019.
21. *jq*: `https://stedolan.github.io/jq/`. Retrieved May 6, 2019.
22. *Splunk*: `https://www.splunk.com/`. Retrieved May 6, 2019.
23. *Datadog*: `https://www.datadoghq.com/`. Retrieved May 6, 2019.
24. *logrus—GoDoc*: `https://godoc.org/github.com/sirupsen/logrus#JSONFormatter`. Retrieved May 6, 2019.
25. *Grafana*: `https://grafana.com/`. Retrieved May 6, 2019.
26. *Bias of bad customer service interactions*: `https://www.marketingcharts.com/digital-28628`. Retrieved May 6, 2019.
27. *Machine Learning on AWS*: `https://aws.amazon.com/machine-learning/`. Retrieved May 6, 2019.
28. *Azure Machine Learning Service*: `https://azure.microsoft.com/en-gb/services/machine-learning-service/`. Retrieved May 6, 2019.
29. *Cloud AI*: `https://cloud.google.com/products/ai/`. Retrieved May 6, 2019.
30. *Cloud Market Share Q4 2018 and Full Year 2018*: `https://www.canalys.com/newsroom/cloud-market-share-q4-2018-and-full-year-2018`. Retrieved May 11, 2019.
31. *Amazon Sagemaker Example*: `https://github.com/awslabs/amazon-sagemaker-examples/blob/master/scientific_details_of_algorithms/ntm_topic_modeling/ntm_wikitext.ipynb`. Retrieved May 11, 2019.
32. *Sagemaker SDK for Go*: `https://docs.aws.amazon.com/sdk-for-go/api/service/sagemaker/`. Retrieved May 11, 2019.

33. *An overview of Sagemaker*: https://www.youtube.com/watch?v=ym7NEYEx9x4. Retrieved May 11, 2019.
34. *Rekognition Go SDK*: https://docs.aws.amazon.com/sdk-for-go/api/service/rekognition/. Retrieved May 11, 2019.
35. *Azure Stream Analytics integration with Azure Machine Learning*: https://docs.microsoft.com/en-us/azure/stream-analytics/stream-analytics-machine-learning-integration-tutorial. Retrieved May 11, 2019.
36. *Azure Go SDK*: https://github.com/Azure/azure-sdk-for-go. Retrieved May 11, 2019.
37. *Consume web service*: https://docs.microsoft.com/en-us/azure/machine-learning/studio/consume-web-services. Retrieved May 11, 2019.
38. *Quickstart: Using Go to call the Text Analytics API*. https://docs.microsoft.com/en-us/azure/cognitive-services/text-analytics/quickstarts/go. Retrieved May 11, 2019.
39. *Cost comparison of deep learning hardware*: https://medium.com/bigdatarepublic/cost-comparison-of-deep-learning-hardware-google-tpuv2-vs-nvidia-tesla-v100-3c63fe56c20f. Retrieved May 11, 2019.
40. *Prediction Overview*: https://cloud.google.com/ml-engine/docs/tensorflow/prediction-overview. Retrieved May 11, 2019.
41. *Google AI Hub*: https://cloud.google.com/ai-hub/. Retrieved May 11, 2019.
42. *Amazon ECR Managed Policies*: https://docs.aws.amazon.com/AmazonECR/latest/userguide/ecr_managed_policies.html. Retrieved May 11, 2019.
43. *App Service - Web App for Containers*: https://azure.microsoft.com/en-gb/services/app-service/containers/. Retrieved May 11, 2019.
44. *Push Docker Image to Private Registry*: https://docs.microsoft.com/en-gb/azure/container-registry/container-registry-get-started-docker-cli. Retrieved May 11, 2019.
45. *Create Docker/Go app on Linux*: https://docs.microsoft.com/en-gb/azure/app-service/containers/quickstart-docker-go. Retrieved May 11, 2019.
46. *Container Registry*: https://cloud.google.com/container-registry/. Retrieved May 11, 2019.
47. *Quickstart for Docker*: https://cloud.google.com/cloud-build/docs/quickstart-docker. Retrieved May 11, 2019.
48. *Mechanical Turk*: https://www.mturk.com/. Retrieved May 15, 2019.
49. *Shrink your Go binaries with this one weird trick*: https://blog.filippo.io/shrink-your-go-binaries-with-this-one-weird-trick/. Retrieved May 16th, 2019.

7
Conclusion - Successful ML Projects

So far in this book, we have focused on how to prepare and use ML algorithms in Go. This included the preparation of data in Chapter 2, *Setting Up the Development Environment*, and the use of data to build models in Chapter 3, *Supervised Learning*, and Chapter 4, *Unsupervised Learning*. We also looked at how to integrate an existing ML model into a Go application in Chapter 5, *Using Pretrained Models*. Finally, we covered how to integrate ML into production systems in Chapter 6, *Deploying Machine Learning Applications*. To conclude, we will take a look at the different stages in a typical project, and how to manage the end-to-end process of developing and deploying a successful ML system.

AI expert Andrej Karparthy has written[1] about how ML can be used to simplify what were previously very complex systems. Often, it is simpler to allow a machine to learn from data than it is to express all the logic we need in code. For example, Google's automatic translation application was simplified from 500,000 lines of conventional code to 500 lines of ML code using a neural network system. Changing from conventional code to a ML system requires different skill sets, and a different approach to software development.

Much of the technical literature on ML focuses on how to optimize or choose models to achieve the best performance, as measured against a test dataset. While this is important in advancing state-of-the-art ML, most real-world projects will succeed or fail against very different criteria. For example, it is crucial to understand how business needs are best translated into ML tasks, what the limitations of your ML systems are, and how best to manage the overall process of designing and maintaining ML applications.

In this chapter, we will cover the following topics:

- When to use ML
- Typical stages in a ML project
- When to combine ML with traditional code

When to use ML

At the outset of any new project, you will need to identify whether ML is the correct approach. This depends on three key factors:

- First of all, it is crucial to understand your business requirements, and whether it can indeed be tackled by ML. Think about what the goals of your project are. For example, do you want to reduce the cost of a process that currently requires significant manual work and cost? Are you trying to create a better experience for your end customer, for example, by adding personalized features that would be too time-consuming to build using traditional code?
- Next, ask yourself whether you have the data required to make your proposed ML system work. If not, how will you acquire the data you need, and what potential issues will need to be solved? For example, you might need to bring together datasets from different areas within your organization, or you may find that privacy issues will impact how you can make appropriate use of your data.

- Finally, consider the limitations of ML and how these might impact your end product. For example, if you are going to use information from a customer database that contains many more men than women, then any ML system that you build from it may show a bias in its output unless you take steps to correct it. Typically, ML systems can generate unpredictable outputs when presented with data that is very different from that used in training and development. If you design a system to trade financial securities, think about what will happen if the input data changes suddenly, for example, following a market crash? How will you make sure that your system behaves safely, and does not emit nonsensical or catastrophic output?

In many cases, you will not be able to know the answers to all of these questions at the start. A good approach in this situation is to start by identifying and building a **proof-of-concept** (**PoC**). Think of this as the simplest and cheapest possible demonstration that you can build of your ML application. With a good PoC, you should be able to do the following:

- Answer questions about whether ML is the right approach, and whether it addresses your business needs.
- Uncover potential problems that you will have to address when building your full system.
- Create a demonstration for stakeholders within your organization, allowing you to get feedback on whether your system will be fit-for-purpose, and what improvements and changes will need to be considered.

> A PoC or **minimum viable product** (**MVP**) is a simple and cheap demonstration of a ML product. Use it to answer questions you have about how your product will work before you spend time and money building a full production system.

Typical stages in a ML project

As we have seen throughout this book, ML is highly dependent on the data that is used for training and testing. For this reason, we find it helpful to view a typical project through the stages in the following diagram, which comes from the **Cross Industry Standard Process for Data Mining** (**CRISP-DM**), a popular method for managing data science projects[3]:

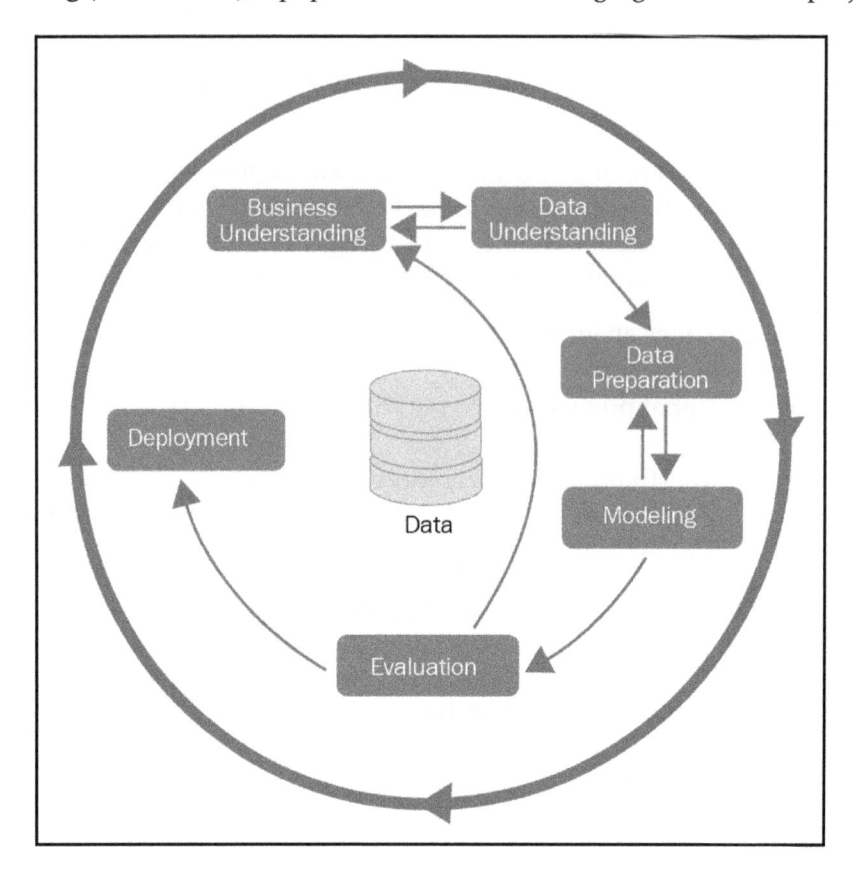

In contrast to some other engineering systems, ML normally never produces perfect output, so, for this reason, projects are often iterative. Refinements to the datasets and models allow you to produce progressively better results, provided they are justified by your business needs.

Business and data understanding

Having decided to use ML, a crucial step in planning your project involves translating your **business success criteria** into **technical requirements** and objectives for the model. For example, what **performance metrics** should you use to build your model, both in terms of its accuracy and other factors, like computational speed and cost? What other systems does your product need to integrate with? Do you need to make sure that its predictions are free from bias, and, if so how, will you test for this?

While business understanding helps you design a product that will be valuable, **data understanding** helps you determine what is possible from the data that you have. By working with your data scientists, you can identify any problems with your datasets, and start to identify promising insights which may form the basis of your model.

Data preparation

As we have seen throughout this book, having access to correctly prepared data is essential when building a ML application. Too often, the challenges in this area of **data engineering** are overlooked, resulting in slow progress as more and more time is spent on ad hoc work to integrate data sources and fix quality issues.

For this reason, it is worth thinking about how you will build your **data pipeline**: where does your data come from, what preprocessing will it require, and where will you store it? What checks should you run on your data to make sure any quality problems get identified quickly, before getting baked-in to a trained model?

A variety of tools now exist to help automate and simplify data pipelines, for example, the Apache Airflow project[4], and managed services such as Google's Cloud Composer[5] and Amazon's AWS data pipeline[6].

> A **data pipeline** is a system that collects, transforms, and stores data in a common format, allowing it to be used as the input to your ML application.

Modelling and evaluation

At this stage, you need to develop, fine-tune, and evaluate models for your data. Usually, there are three options regarding how to do this:

- Use an off-the-shelf ML solution with your own data. For example, Google Vision[7] provides an API for a fully managed image classification system. Often, these services are a good way to get fast results at the PoC stage, but should be approached with caution on bigger projects. Because you have not trained the model yourself, it is often difficult to be sure that it captures the important features of your own data.
- Take an existing open source model and retrain/customize it for your own purposes. For example, if you want to build a system that detects objects in images, it makes sense to leverage all the R&D effort that large organizations have already put into this problem[8]. You can use these models to give you a head-start, and then retrain them on your own datasets.
- Develop and train a model from scratch using the techniques that we learned about in Chapter 3, *Supervised Learning*, and Chapter 4, *Unsupervised Learning*. While this can be the most time-consuming approach, it often yields the best results if your problem is unique to your organization.

Regardless of the option you choose, it is important to ensure that your model's development and testing are **reproducible**. Make sure it is documented, and that both the model and its data requirements are captured in a version control system. Doing so will allow different team members to work on the same model and be confident in getting the same results.

> A **reproducible model** is one that has sufficient code and documentation to allow it to be retrained easily on the same dataset that was used during development. It should also include the version numbers of all the software libraries and frameworks that it depends on.

Deployment

A ML model is only useful if it can be deployed into a production system. In `Chapter 6`, *Deploying Machine Learning Applications*, we explored techniques for how to achieve this in Go. Following these techniques will allow you to deploy your model reliably. As you start to iterate through the project stages to improve your product, it is also important to track the different model versions as they enter production. One option is to check all of your saved models into a version control system such as Git, although this can be problematic if your model contains large files. Another option is to use **Data Version Control** (**DVC**), which is able to track the code, models, and datasets that they depend on.

When to combine ML with traditional code

While most of this book has focused on how to write and use ML code, you will have also noticed that a lot of traditional, non-ML code is needed to support what we have done. Much of this is hidden inside the software libraries we have used, but there are cases where you may need to add to this.

One example is where you need to enforce certain constraints on your model output, for instance, to handle an edge case or implement some safety-critical constraints. Suppose you are writing software for a self-driving car: you might use ML to process image data from the cars cameras, but when it comes to actuating the vehicles steering, engine, and brake controls, you will most likely need to use traditional code to ensure that the car is controlled safely. Similarly, unless your ML system is trained to handle unexpected data inputs, for example, from a failed sensor, then you will want to add logic to deal with these cases. Make sure that you test your models with outlier data and edge cases before deployment so that you understand the circumstances under which its performance will degrade.

In all real-world systems, you need to think carefully about what you have trained your ML model to do, what its limitations are, and how to make sure your end-to-end system behaves as expected.

Summary

In this book, you have learned about many important techniques that are required to develop ML applications in Go, and deploy them as production systems. The best way to develop your knowledge is with hands-on experience, so dive in and start adding ML software into your own Go applications. The skills you have learned here will allow you to start adding cutting-edge ML capabilities to the projects that you are working on.

ML is a rapidly evolving field with new algorithms and datasets being published every week, both by academics and technology companies. We recommend that you read the technical blogs, papers, and code repositories that cover this research, many of which we have referenced throughout this book. You might find a new state-of-the-art model that solves a problem you have been working on, waiting for you to implement it in Go.

Further readings

1. https://medium.com/@karpathy/software-2-0-a64152b37c35. Retrieved May 17, 2019.
2. https://jack-clark.net/2017/10/09/import-ai-63-google-shrinks-language-translation-code-from-500000-to-500-lines-with-ai-only-25-of-surveyed-people-believe-automationbetter-jobs/. Retrieved May 17, 2019.
3. https://pdfs.semanticscholar.org/48b9/293cfd4297f855867ca278f7069abc6a9c24.pdf. Retrieved May 18, 2019.
4. https://airflow.apache.org/. Retrieved May 18, 2019.
5. https://cloud.google.com/composer/. Retrieved May 18, 2019.
6. https://aws.amazon.com/datapipeline/. Retrieved May 18, 2019.
7. https://cloud.google.com/vision/. Retrieved May 18, 2019.
8. https://github.com/tensorflow/models/tree/master/research/object_detection. Retrieved May 18, 2019.
9. https://dvc.org/. Retrieved May 22, 2019.
10. https://becominghuman.ai/how-to-version-control-your-machine-learning-task-ii-d37da60ef570. Retrieved May 22, 2019.

Other Books You May Enjoy

If you enjoyed this book, you may be interested in these other books by Packt:

Go Machine Learning Projects
Xuanyi Chew

ISBN: 9781788993401

- Set up a machine learning environment with Go libraries
- Use Gonum to perform regression and classification
- Explore time series models and decompose trends with Go libraries
- Clean up your Twitter timeline by clustering tweets
- Learn to use external services for your machine learning needs

Hands-On Go Programming
Tarik Guney

ISBN: 9781789531756

- Manipulate string values and escape special characters
- Work with dates, times, maps, and arrays
- Handle errors and perform logging
- Explore files and directories
- Handle HTTP requests and responses

Leave a review - let other readers know what you think

Please share your thoughts on this book with others by leaving a review on the site that you bought it from. If you purchased the book from Amazon, please leave us an honest review on this book's Amazon page. This is vital so that other potential readers can see and use your unbiased opinion to make purchasing decisions, we can understand what our customers think about our products, and our authors can see your feedback on the title that they have worked with Packt to create. It will only take a few minutes of your time, but is valuable to other potential customers, our authors, and Packt. Thank you!

Index

A

accuracy
  measuring 59
  precision measures 59, 61
  recall measures 59, 61
  ROC curves 62
Amazon AI Services 132, 133
Amazon Sagemaker 131
Amazon Web Services 129, 131
area under curve (AUC) 62
Artificial Intelligence (AI) 5
Azure Cognitive Services 134
Azure ML Studio 134

B

backpropagation 71
base models 79
baseline 57
binary classification 63
body mass index, exploring with gonum/plot
  data series distributions 34, 36
  data, loading 33, 34
  example 32
  gonum, installing 32
  gonum/plot, installing 32

C

centroid 85
classification algorithm 8
classification
  about 54, 56
  accuracy, measuring 59
  logistic classifier 56, 58
  multi-class models 63, 64, 66
  non-linear model 66, 68, 69
clustering 84, 85, 87

clustering algorithm 83
continuous delivery (CD) 113
continuous delivery feedback loop
  about 113
  deployment 116
  development portion 114
  monitoring 121, 122
  testing 114, 115
continuous integration/continuous deployment (CI/CD) 18
convolutional layers 72
Cross Industry Standard Process for Data Mining (CRISP-DM) 144

D

data engineering 145
data normalization methods, in Gota
  mean normalization 42
  rescaling 42
  standardization 43
data pipeline 145
Data Version Control (DVC) 147
data, preprocessing with Gota
  categorical variables, used, for encoding data 47, 49
  columns, converting 40
  columns, removing 39
  columns, renaming 39
  data normalization 42, 44
  data, loading into Gota 38
  example 37
  training/validation subsets, obtaining by sampling 45, 46
  unwanted data, filtering 41, 42
deep learning model
  architecture 73
deep learning, using TensorFlow API for Go

about 102, 103
inputs, creating to TensorFlow Model 108, 109
pretrained TensorFlow model, importing 106, 108
TensorFlow, installing 104, 105
deep learning
  about 70
  neural networks 71
deep neural network 71
deployment models, for cloud application
  Infrastructure as a Service (IaaS) 128
  Platform as a Service (PaaS) 128, 131
deployment models
  for model applications 128
deployment, continuous delivery feedback loop
  dependencies 116, 117, 118
  model persistence 119, 120, 121
dimensionality reduction 9
DistBelief 103

E

eigenvalues 89
eigenvectors 89
Elastic Compute (EC2) 129
Elastic Container Registry (ECR) 129
ensemble model 79
epoch 74
estimation 8

F

feature scaling 42
focal loss 17
FreeBSD
  Go, installing 22
fully-connected layer 72

G

general intelligence 83
Go
  advantages 9, 10
  installing 22
  installing, on FreeBSD 22
  installing, on Linux 22
  installing, on macOS 22
  installing, on Windows 23

mature ecosystem 10, 11
ML applications, writing in 9
running, with gophernotes 23, 24
Google Cloud
  about 130, 134
  AI building blocks 135
  AI platform 135
GOPATH
  about 23
  reference 23
gophernotes
  used, for running Go 23, 24
Gota
  used, for preprocessing data 37
graphs 103

H

heuristic 7
hidden layer 71
high bias 69
high variance 69
HTTP
  used, for invoking Python model 100, 102
huber loss 16

I

Infrastructure as a Service (IaaS)
  about 18, 116, 128
  Amazon Web Services 129
  Google Cloud 130
  Microsoft Azure 130

J

JavaScript Object Notation (JSON) 97
Jupyter 14

K

K-means algorithm 85
Keras 71
kernel function
  using 67

L

labeled pair 8
labeled set 8
learning rate 74
LIBSVM library 67
linear model 56
linear regression 78
Linux
  Go, installing 22
logarithmic loss 17
logistic classifier 56, 58
logistic function 73
loss 74
loss metrics
  about 16
  focal loss 17
  huber loss 16
  logarithmic loss 17
  mean absolute error (MAE) 16
  mean square error (MSE) 16

M

machine learning (ML)
  about 5, 6, 7, 21, 93, 113
  combining, with traditional code 147
  using 142, 143
machine learning project
  business success criteria 145
  data preparation 145
  data understanding 145
  deployment 147
  evaluation 146
  modelling 146
  stages 144
macOS
  Go, installing 22
mean absolute error (MAE) 16, 78
mean normalization 42
mean square error (MSE) 16, 78
Mechanical Turk
  reference 132
Microsoft Azure 130
Microsoft Internet Information Services (IIS) 130
minimum viable product (MVP) 143

ML algorithms
  supervised learning problems 8
  types 7
  unsupervised learning problems 9
ML applications
  deployment applications 128
  writing, in Go 9
ML development life cycle
  about 11
  algorithm, selecting 14, 15
  data, acquiring 13
  data, exploring 13
  data, preparing 15, 16
  deploying 18
  integrating 18
  issues, defining 12, 13
  objectives, defining 12, 13
  re-validating 18
  testing 17
  training 16
  validating 17
MNIST Fashion dataset 54
monitoring, continuous delivery feedback loop
  feedback 125, 126, 127
  metrics, capturing 124, 125
  structured logging 123
multi-class models 63, 64, 66
multi-domain sentiment dataset, reviews example
  about 25
  contents, parsing into Struct 27, 28
  data, loading into Gota dataframe 29
  dataset files, loading 26, 27
  dataset, downloading 25
  directory, initializing 25
  phrases for reviews, finding 30, 31

N

neural networks
  about 71, 72
  training 74
non-linear model 66, 68, 69

O

one-hot encoding 48
os/exec

used, for invoking Python model 97, 99, 100
outliers 41
overfitting 17, 69, 70

P

perceptron 71
Platform as a Service (PaaS)
  about 18, 116, 131
  Amazon Web Services (AWS) 131
  Google Cloud 134
  Microsoft Azure 133
polyglot approach
  adopting 95, 96
prediction algorithms 8
principal component analysis (PCA) 83, 88, 89, 90, 91
proof-of-concept (PoC) 143
Python model
  invoking, with HTTP 100, 102
  invoking, with os/exec 97, 99, 100

R

radial basis function (RBF) kernel 68
random forest regression 79
receiver operating characteristic (ROC) curve 62
recommender system 6
rectified linear unit (ReLU) 73
regression 8, 75, 76
regression models 80
regression, types
  linear regression 78
  random forest regression 79

Remote Procedure Call (RPC) 100
reproducible model 146
rescaling 42
risk register 121

S

saved GoML model
  restoring 94, 95
softmax regression
  using, in goml/linear 63
standard output (STDOUT) 97
standardization 43
supervised learning
  classification 54, 56
support vector machine (SVM) model 66, 68, 69

T

tanh function 73
TensorFlow 71
tensors 103
test set 56
training set 56

U

unbalanced dataset 59
underfitting 69, 70
unsupervised learning 83

W

Windows
  Go, installing 23

Lightning Source UK Ltd.
Milton Keynes UK
UKHW031951250619
345010UK00006B/121/P